WEALTH BEYOND THE NUMBERS

A Simple But Powerful Financial And Life Plan For Living Your Best Life.

By Tom Suvansri

Perennial Pride

700 Canal Street, 1st Floor

Stamford, Connecticut 06902

Email: tom@perennialpride.com

Website: perennialpride.com

Phone: 203-918-6424

Cover design by Cyberdogz
Cover image used provided by iStock

Printed in the United States of America

This book is dedicated to all those who want to learn a better way to gain financial control, to grow, and create wealth and impact that will last for generations.

Take care, brush your hair.

Tom Suwansri

Contents

Acknowledgments

"In the long run, we shape our lives, and we shape ourselves. The process never ends until we die. And the choices we make are ultimately our own responsibility."

- Eleanor Roosevelt

A simple thank you to my family who gave me the courage to write this book. The original goal and motivation behind all this was to simply collect all the great information that I've used throughout my journey, so that I could pass that along to my kids. My hope is that this will get through to them and all future generations of Suvansris.

I'd also like to thank the many mentors and colleagues I've worked with along the way and especially, to the the late great R. Nelson Nash for sharing this concept with all of us. *Becoming Your Own Banker* has cultivated a path for several people and hopefully will continue to inspire the growth of financial freedom.

Finally, thanks to my amazing wife for supporting and believing in me. I am a firm believer that without your patience and support, I would not be where I am today.

Key Steps

Although I have provided a conventional table of contents, you may find it easier to navigate this book by flipping through the **15 Key Steps** placed sequentially throughout the manuscript. The Key Steps are my way of sharing with you the most valuable lessons I've learned – often the hard way – about money and life. Feel free to jump around and share these lessons with the people you care about most. If you get nothing else out of this book, make sure you understand this: Our time on earth is very limited, so make the most of it.

INTRO

Introduction To Tom

"A life is not important except in the impact it has on other lives."
– Jackie Robinson

When I sat down to think about the theme of this guide, I realized I wanted to share my financial journey with you so you could see how it has enabled me to accumulate both financial wealth and a sense of abundance in all areas of my life – health, relationships, family, etc. I call that "***wealth beyond the numbers.***"

Wealth isn't just about the amount of money you have in your investment or retirement accounts. It's about the abundance of anything you want in life. It took me a long while to realize this, but my own financial journey enabled me – eventually – to see that gaining control over my own wealth would allow me to discover what I truly valued in life. It would also allow me to build "wealth" in all areas of my life, not just the financial areas. That's what I want to share with you in this guide. I hope the lessons I learned on my financial journey will help you discover your own personal definition of wealth and utilize my strategies to help you build it.

As I began writing this guide and assessing my journey to financial freedom and success, I was struck by how many resources and "mentors" have shaped my vision for personal growth and my worldview. They've not only provided me with the wisdom to succeed but have given me the courage to move forward on a journey that originally frightened me a great deal.

I've made best efforts to highlight those luminaries in the pages that follow.

While my editors and I have put a lot of effort into sharing my life lessons in a logical order, you should feel free to skip around. At the end of each chapter, you will see **Financial Footprints** you can follow to put the advice within each chapter into action. You will also find a **Key Learnings** summary at the conclusion of each chapter.

Feel free to skip around this guide at your leisure. However you read it, I urge you to review the Financial Footprints and Key Learnings within each chapter before moving on to the next chapter. It's all part of helping you achieve the wealth you desire in your financial and personal life.

MY STORY

Like many parents, my folks wanted to provide the best for their children. Born and raised in Thailand, they came to the United States as young adults to seek better opportunities – but not at the same time.

After completing medical school in Thailand, my father braved the trip to the U.S. first to start his residency. On top of a rigorous training program, he had to overcome barriers of language and race as he eventually finished his training.

It took several years for my father to get settled in the U.S., but eventually my mother and my sister came over, and a few years after that my brother and I were born. Through persistence and dedication, my parents established a thriving family medical practice here. Even though they were well educated and making lots of money, they were not financially literate. They never learned the basics of protecting, managing and growing the burgeoning wealth that was coming into their lives.

I grew up in an upper-middle-class community in the comfortable New Jersey suburbs. It was a wonderful environment in which to come of age. It was not only a safe community with excellent schools but, unlike many suburbs, it was very diverse. That allowed me – a shy boy of Asian descent to thrive socially, athletically, and sometimes academically. Best of all, it gave me the freedom to explore, learn and make mistakes.

My parents were always very busy running a successful family medical practice. My siblings and I had all the food, shelter, and clothing we could ever need, and they often showered us with gifts. I sensed I was fortunate, but I didn't really understand how much more fortunate I was than many other kids growing up in the U.S. and certainly around the world. Some might say I was spoiled. My parents funded most of my undergraduate education, but I didn't think that was a big deal. I was expected to go to college and to graduate with at least an undergraduate degree before pursuing graduate studies. Besides, college then was ***way*** more affordable than it is today, so financing it was not a big deal for people in our community.

But beneath the surface, my parents were in a lot of pain. Although they were good at hiding their financial and marriage troubles for quite some time, I started noticing disturbing cracks in the foundation as I came into the final semester of my MBA program. Out of the blue, I noticed my personal credit was shot. I couldn't think of what I had done to trash my credit since I paid my credit card bills for the most part on time and hadn't run up any other debts. It turns out my mother had to borrow nearly $50,000 under my name just to get by. She and my father owed a massive amount of back taxes from the medical practice. They could no longer get credit under their own name even though the practice was bringing in lots of money, and they desperately needed money to get the IRS off their backs.

I was in shock. Once the anger and disbelief subsided, my siblings and I started tackling my parents' financial problems head-on, and those hard-learned lessons put me on the path to where I am today. It was a very difficult period in my life, but I realize now it was one of the greatest "gifts" my parents ever gave to me: having a true purpose in life. It was much more valuable than any of the video games and toys they paid for.

My parents did the best they could with the information and education they had, but it wasn't enough to manage a thriving medical practice responsibly. From that day forward, I vowed never to go through the pain they endured with their financial situation wealth – and to help others avoid making those same mistakes.

Like many people, I followed the conventional "smart money" advice when I was younger. I thought I was doing everything right, but essentially, I was obsessed with making money and being successful, which in my eyes was the same thing. Yet I never felt fulfilled.

It was only after I matured a little and gained some life experiences that I realized: having money and wealth doesn't guarantee success and happiness – wealth is simply a tool to get you on the path to fulfillment. Money alone should never be the reason you do anything in life. My fascination with money was not driven by a need to acquire all kinds of things. It was driven more from watching my parents' financial failures and vowing never to make the same mistakes they did.

Sadly, my parents' story is not just an immigrants' tale. It happens to many successful families in America. They work very hard to accumulate massive wealth, but never have the opportunity to enjoy it – and neither do their families.

MONEY: A TABOO SUBJECT

As a family, we never really talked about money because my parents weren't very financially literate. It's not that we were underprivileged as kids. We never lacked basic necessities. We always had nice clothes, toys, and bicycles. We took plenty of vacations, including Disney World and Atlantic City. My parents even funded our education (albeit college was much more affordable in those days).

But financial turmoil was lurking just below the surface. While my parents' medical practice generated ***LOTS*** of revenue, they didn't save much of it. Worse, they invested in things they didn't understand and couldn't control. As a result, they allowed their wealth to shrink substantially due to taxes, fees, and other hidden "wealth eroders" that left them with next to nothing.

My siblings and I weren't aware of my parents' situation until that memorable day I reviewed my credit report. I swore I would never let myself end up in the same financial straits that my parents were in. I started reading everything I could about investing and being smarter with my money. It started with classics such as *The Millionaire Next Door*, which taught me how to be frugal with my money. Yes, this approach could work to create some wealth, but over time I realized I didn't want to completely sacrifice today for tomorrow. Of course, this was in the late 1990s, when actively managed mutual funds were all the rage. Then the 2000 market crash occurred, and before my portfolio had fully recovered, we had the 2008-2009 financial crisis. Wham! Some of those hits I took to my portfolio hurt worse than any collision I ever had on the college football field. I knew there had to be a better way to own and control my financial future and my life so that I could become financially independent and direct the future I wanted.

DISCLAIMER: The author has neither a financial nor promotional interest in any of the books, resources, products or services mentioned throughout this guide.

I read everything I could about investment alternatives to the stock market, primarily real estate. Robert Kiyosaki's *Rich Dad Poor Dad* especially made an impression on me; it wasn't like anything I had read before in my education or heard from my financial advisor. I discovered that your CASH FLOW was more important than your NET WORTH. Whether you're a salaried worked or self-employed, you need to treat your wealth as a business and be a real investor of assets that build cash flow – not just someone who contributes to a 401(k), IRA or SEP.

As I continued my investment education, I discovered many other ways to invest in real estate and learned how the wealthy often build their vast sums. They don't simply accumulate dollars in accounts, hoping their money will grow; they leverage the resources of others to expand their control of assets in order to generate cash flow. Fortunately, I'm a lifelong learner. I never get tired of discovering what's out there, available from the best and brightest thinkers inside and outside our industry. Kim Butler's short but powerful book *Financial Planning Has Failed* is a great work that addresses some of the common problems with the typical approach to financial planning. It also introduces sound economic principles and unique life insurance strategies using whole life insurance – including some I wasn't even aware of when I first picked up a copy. I did have some cash value built up in my own account, even though the policies were not designed optimally, and I realized that it never lost value over the course of my owning it. Through my research, networking and introductions, I found my way to Kim Butler, originator of **PEM** (***the*** *Prosperity Economics Movement*), and things progressed from there.

I learned how best to finance things (I recommend Nelson Nash's *Becoming Your Own Banker* for this). I learned about how money truly works and how various mainstream financial institutions make their money. I was using some of the same strategies for my own financial life but had never come across PEM with other advisors. PEM opened up a new world for me!

Now that my worldview has expanded, I can see how it's possible to gain more freedom and control over one's wealth, and how I can help future generations in my family continue this growth for themselves and impact the world around them I very much want to do the same for all of you reading this guide.

Let me tell you more about the lessons I learned on my journey. Spoiler alert: it's not about striving for massive sums of wealth; it's about striving to become the best versions of ourselves to live a life that's fulfilling and to have the biggest impact on the world around us. What I've learned on my own journey has helped me feel not only more financially successful but more successful in all areas of life. I've learned over time that feeling wealthy is not just about having lots of money; it's about having a sense of abundance in all key areas of life (health, relationships, spirituality, finances, etc.). That is what true wealth is.

Life can be incredibly chaotic for people who are trying to balance their work or business with family responsibilities, including childcare and/or eldercare, plus trying to stay fit while also giving back to their community or religious organization.

While many people strive to achieve work/life balance, there's really no such thing if you're in relentless pursuit of wealth to support your increasingly complicated lifestyle. Chances are, you're like I used to be. You're letting external pressures and other people's expectations dictate how you live your life instead of reflecting on what you care about most.

It's easy to get stuck on the proverbial "hamster wheel" in which you're mindlessly commuting long distances to a job you don't love, every weekday, for no reason other than to pay the bills and have healthcare. Everything else in your life (family, friends, errands, kids activities, hobbies, community, faith, etc.) gets squeezed into the weekend, which inevitably evaporates in the blink of an eye. Before you know it, it's Sunday night and that dark cloud of doom descends on you again.

Don't you deserve more enjoyment and fulfillment in life each and every day?

Of course, you do! So why aren't you taking steps to change that equation?

WHAT LIONS TEACH US

It all starts with learning strategies for being successful and ensuring they are passed down to your heirs. Now, I've always been fascinated with lions – especially how they seek to secure and protect their territory and provide for their pride. I was fascinated by jungle-related books as a kid, and it's amazing how often my various sports teams were named after some derivation of lion. Eventually, I moved on to Penn State University (home of the Nittany Lions) for graduate school. See the pattern?

Being the king of the jungle takes courage, power, intelligence and collaboration, and the role must be maintained for numerous generations to protect the family lineage. Lions not only survive, but they thrive and become a powerful force in nature. That is why the lion is an essential part of our firm's brand and identity, Perennial Pride. The mighty lion takes control of its situation and has the freedom to pursue its goals on its own terms, not on anyone else's.

In the wild, big cats use scent to mark their territory. By learning strategies I'll share with you throughout this book, you'll be

able to expand and protect your own territory by using financial "scent markers" to help you achieve financial sense. This is part of the reason the proud lion is so important to our firm's identity.

TIME FAMINE

It turns out that time (not money) is the scarcest resource for successful people like you. Unfortunately, we don't know when our time will run out. To live our best lives, we need to use our time as efficiently as we can, and that means prioritizing how we spend each and every day. With the news, social media, and streaming services constantly competing for your attention, it's easy to let your valuable time slip through the cracks – never to be seen again.

We face many headwinds on the journey through life and dealing with constant "time famine" is just one of them. Society pressures us to focus on what we think we're supposed to be doing (e.g., getting a good job, buying a big house, moving to a prestigious neighborhood, putting our kids in private school, purchasing a fancy car, going on luxurious vacations) just so we can post these status symbols on social media to make our peers and neighbors jealous. But in this endless game of one-upmanship, we rarely feel fulfilled, even when we think we are winning.

AS THE OLD SAYING GOES:
"Even if you win the rat race, you're still a rat!"

The same empty feeling can apply to your finances, even if your bank account seems well-stocked. Trust me, we hear this all the time from new clients when we first start working with them. As you start to acquire more income and assets, it can feel as though everyone is competing for your cash and trying to convince you to give up control so others can manage your money. Unfortunately, when you give up financial control to others, you'll have a hard time reaching your potential. That's because significant wealth is being lost along the way.

Conventional wisdom tells us that in order to reach our financial goals, we have to take on some risk, and we need the so-called financial advisors at large financial institutions to make those decisions for us. You DON'T.

In the pages that follow, I'll show you why. There is absolutely no reason why successful people like you should ever have to leave significant wealth on the table and pay unnecessary fees, interest and costs so other people (banks, financial institutions, etc.) can enjoy your hard-earned wealth, instead of you and your family.

FINANCIAL TAILWINDS

As you pursue your life goals, wouldn't you rather have tailwinds than headwinds?

To get you started on the right path, I'm going to share several Key Steps to follow so you can live your best life and more easily reach your financial goals. I call these steps your "financial tailwinds." They will push you along at just the right pace and in just the right direction to let you reach your goals on a timetable you're comfortable with, so you have the freedom to live your life on your terms.

You'll find this process a lot more enjoyable than fighting financial headwinds all day long.

NOTE: I don't promise a quick fix for a more fulfilling life even though that is what many people seem to be looking for these days. As with so many things in life, there are very few miracle cures and instant solutions for achieving financial freedom. Instead, getting there will require patience, hard work, discipline and a commitment to continuous learning. This journey is not for the lazy or indifferent who simply want to hand off their money to others to manage.

I know you're ready to accept the challenge.

This book is divided into four key chapters that align with our firm's philosophy for living your best life and creating an impact to last for generations:

Chapter 1. Own Your Response and Be Accountable

Chapter 2. Build Self-Awareness and Create Your Unique Impact

Chapter 3. Secure True and Ultimate Freedom

Chapter 4. See the Good

Within each chapter, I'll share simple but powerful lifestyle strategies to move you closer to a life of fulfillment. These aren't just pie-in-the-sky aspirational goals. Each lifestyle strategy is bolstered by a sound financial strategy that makes sure you have the resources to put it into action for a better life outcome. Again, we call those strategies **Financial Footprints**.Throughout the book, I'll also weave in 15 Key Steps that are designed to help you live your best life. Many of these steps will sound familiar to Perennial Pride clients.

CHAPTER ONE

Own Your Response And Be Accountable

"Freedom is the will to be responsible for ourselves."
- Friedrich Nietzsche

Many people believe that happiness and fulfillment in life are driven by external factors such as how much money you make or how successful you feel at your job or business. For some people, it's about fame (or lack thereof). I used to think that way as well. But as I've matured, I've learned that happiness and fulfillment are derived from a commitment to lifelong personal growth, contribution to others, becoming the best version of myself and living life based on my core values – not based on external factors such as peer pressure, societal pressure and keeping up with the Joneses.

That's why taking personal responsibility for your life is absolutely essential for living your best life. Ask most people what they truly want in life, and you'll rarely get a clear answer, if anything at all. Most people don't think about why they do what they do every day – they just do it.

Most will simply explain their purpose in life in terms of what they think society wants us to believe is important: get a good job, buy a house, raise your kids right and retire into the sunset. But how often do most people reflect on their current lives and determine if it's the path they wanted to take? Not many. Do they experience joy, fulfillment, and purpose each day? Generally, no.

But that doesn't mean you have to accept it. Knowing who you are and what you want is absolutely essential. Then it's up to you take the necessary actions to make it happen.

"Get busy living or get busy dying."– Shawshank Redemption

I experienced all of this firsthand. I followed the standard approach as I worked in corporate America for over 20 years at a good company with benefits. I tolerated the commute, which took nearly three hours a day, so that I could make a living to support my family. Yes, it helped me provide for my family, but as I reflect on those years, I can say it wasn't personally fulfilling. It was a means to the end. I won't knock people who go this route, but I know my life has more meaning now than ever before.

Only once I took the steps to explore a new opportunity to open up my own financial practice did it really click for me. Although scary, becoming an entrepreneur allowed me to build something for myself that I could own and control for my future while serving others with my expertise and care. It took courage and personal responsibility to take the necessary steps and face the many challenges that stood in the way. This has led me down a different path – a path that has led to a more fulfilling and satisfying life of service. But it all started with taking responsibility for my life and creating the vision for my future that I'd dreamed about.

KEY STEP 1: CLARIFY YOUR VISION

When asked what they want their future to look like, most people can't easily describe it. *Strategic coach Dan Sullivan*, a leading motivational speaker and coach for entrepreneurs, uses a technique called the "The R-Factor Question," in which he asks: If we were meeting here three years from today, what needs to have happened in your life, both personally and professionally, for you to feel happy with your progress?

One way to answer the R-Factor Question is keep a regular journal in which you jot down thoughts every day about what your ideal future looks like. Ask yourself: "How would I want life to look, feel, smell?" and "Who would I be with, and what would my days look like?

A great example of this comes from the new hit movie *King Richard: American Dreams* about Richard Williams (Will Smith), the enigmatic father of tennis superstars Venus and Serena Williams, who taught his daughters to follow a plan every day and envision what it would be like to become Wimbledon champions despite their humble beginnings in inner-city Los Angeles. Skip to the one-minute mark for *this clip*.

Now that you've put a framework around your ideal future, here comes the hard part: assessing where you are in the key areas of life (business, financial, physical, mental, family, spiritual, lifestyle, relationships). Trust me, this is not a 15-minute exercise. The Life Assessment grid below will help you determine where you are in various aspects of your life so you can chart a confident path forward. Knowing where you are is the first step in taking responsibility for the direction in your life.

AREA	SCORE (1-10)
Business	
Financial	
Physical	
Mental	
Family	
Spiritual	
Lifestyle	
Relationships	

Source: Adapted from Darren Hardy

As you assess each key area of your life (above), be as honest as you can about how things are going and whether you think you could be making improvements in several of those areas. Is your business or career where you want it to be? Are your finances adequate to let you live the life you desire? Do you have the relationships with your family you dreamed of? Don't worry about how others might be answering these questions or what society "expects of you." It's your life. The more honesty you bring to this exercise, the higher your potential upside.

If you're like most people, you're very strong in a few areas, not too bad in many areas, and lacking in a few others. Where are the biggest gaps you're seeing? Look at the areas in which you gave yourself the highest score. Are those the areas that are most important to you? Are those areas where you are spending the bulk of your time and resources?

If you don't feel like the key areas of your life are in alignment with your goals and values, you're not alone. But once you can see the reality of where you are across the various aspects of your life, you can then prioritize where to focus. I know these can be big, existential questions. Start by picking the three most important areas of your life where you want to see improvement. For each of those three areas, ask yourself:

1. "Who do I want to become?"
2. "What do I want to achieve?"
3. "What things must I stop doing, and what things should I start doing?"

Ideally, you want to be close to 8-10 with your rating in each area, but depending on where you are, progress is the key.

Now, this next step is a little tougher. Ask yourself: "What would it take, within reason, to get to a level of 8-10 in each area of my Life Assessment?"

Areas Lagging In My Life	Steps Needed To Improve

Source: Perennial Pride, 2022

For more about improving your scores, see Darren Hardy's book *Design Your Best Year Ever*. It includes exercises for identifying where you are, where you want to go and the actions/goals you need to implement in order to get there. Although identifying those goals is very important, prioritizing them is the key to reaching them. And that will require focus and discipline. Sorry, no shortcuts or "life hacks" here.

FINANCIAL FOOTPRINTS

As you'll see throughout this book, the second part of each section discusses the Financial Footprints you'll need to follow to put the strategies I share with you into action. I recommend first mapping out the lifetime goals you have for yourself and your family. Then you'll need a financial plan to get you there. At this stage, you'll want to take a complete picture of your financial life and then ask yourself if you're on track to reaching your short-term, mid-term and long-term goals. If your answer is NO, that's okay. Read on for ways to close the gap(s).

The LEAP Model (*Lifetime Economic Acceleration Process™*) developed by Robert Castiglione, provides a good framework for looking at your entire financial life from five unique viewpoints:

1. Protections
2. Savings
3. Growth
4. Debt
5. Cash Flow

Take a minute to fill in the boxes below to the best of your ability:

	Where Am I Now?	Where Do I Want To Be?
My Protections		
My Savings		
My Growth		
My Debt		
My Cash Flow		

Source: Perennial Pride, 2022

Here are some basic guidelines to follow.

1. Protections: Strive to have the maximum protections for your assets, income and life.
2. Savings: Secure at least six months of liquid savings. Continue to save at least 15% of your income.
3. Growth: Maximize investments in things you can control and reduce risk of loss.
4. Debt: Ensure any debt is good debt that can help you grow wealth.
5. Cash Flow: Understand where your money is going and determine if it's serving you optimally.

Here's a handy checklist of important documents to help you organize your financial life and better assess how you're doing.

Check Box As You Gather Each Document:

[ ] Personal Income Tax Returns

[ ] Paying Stub(s) For You And Your Spouse
Showing Deductions From Gross Income

[ ] Wills and Trust Documents

[ ] All Personal Insurance Policies

- [ ] Automobile Policies (Include Declarations Of Coverage)
- [ ] Homeowner's or Renter's Policy (Include Declarations Of Coverage)
- [ ] Disability Income Policies
- [ ] Hospitalization and Major Medical Policies
- [ ] Life Insurance Policies (For All Members Of Your Family)
  - Annual Statements / - Loan Statements

[ ] Any Other Types Of Insurance Policies

[ ] Most Recent Government Plan Statements

[ ] Most Recent Mortgage Statements

[ ] Employer Provided Group Benefits For You And Your Spouse
(Please Include A Printout Of Specific Coverage's If Available)

[ ] Current Account Statements (For Savings, Retirement, Investments, etc.)

For Business Owners Only:

[ ] Business Life Insurance Policies

[ ] Business Income Tax Returns

[ ] Business Financial Statements

[ ] Buy - Sell Agreements

[ ] Business Agreements (ie: Key Person, Deferred Compensation, etc.)

The idea is to be honest with yourself about where you currently are in each of those five key areas compared to where you'd like to be. Even if you don't feel good about where you are currently in each area, understanding your current state will help you forge the path forward to what you wish to accomplish.

A Gallup survey found that only *three in 10 Americans have a long-term financial plan*. And the Employee Benefit Research Institute found that more than *two-thirds of Americans (70%)* think the main way to ensure a comfortable retirement is to keep working.

As I've always said... ***"Hope Is Not A Strategy."***

Don't fall into that trap. Ask yourself what you want to accomplish financially in the short term, medium term and long term. For instance:

- **Short-term goals** include setting a budget, reducing debt, starting an emergency fund and securing maximum protections.
- **Medium-term goals** include funding home and college, making investments, and growing in work or business.
- **Long-term goals** need to be focused on retirement and legacy planning.

What are things you want to do more of or less of?

___

___

___

How would you define financial success?

___

___

___

What are your views about retirement?

___

___

___

If you're not liking what you see, where do you see the biggest gaps?

____

____

____

____

____

The financial lives of Americans are typically upside down: more of their resources are directed to growing their assets in areas they cannot control, while their financial future is exposed to significant risk.

This is where the **Hierarchy of Wealth**, developed by *Paradigm Life*, can be a great tool for ensuring that your financial foundation is built solidly and can withstand the unexpected shocks we encounter from time to time.

Did you know there is a way to build wealth without exposing yourself to excessive risk and to gain more control over your money than in qualified retirement plans and stock market investments?

Just like Maslow's Hierarchy of Needs for personal survival and fulfillment, there is a natural hierarchy for meeting your financial needs. Fulfill the most essential needs first, before pursuing any other comfort goals or aspirational financial goals. The first step in the Hierarchy of Wealth is to secure your financial foundation through a **Wealth Maximization Account™**. Your WMA is a properly structured whole life insurance tool that provides access to cash value, tax advantages, compound interest, and other benefits that help grow and protect your wealth.

In essence, the Hierarchy of Wealth is a way to balance control and risk in your financial life. Conventional wisdom is that you need to take on greater risk (e.g., stocks) in order to achieve higher returns on your money. However, if you have better control of your assets, you can actually reduce your level of risk while still receiving sizable returns. Many people start thinking about investments before they build a solid financial foundation. Unfortunately, when a storm hits, a house with a weak foundation can come crumbling down. And as we've seen, financial storms often come when we least expect them.

Don't make that mistake.

The Hierarchy of Wealth is a better way to preserve your assets and achieve your goals.

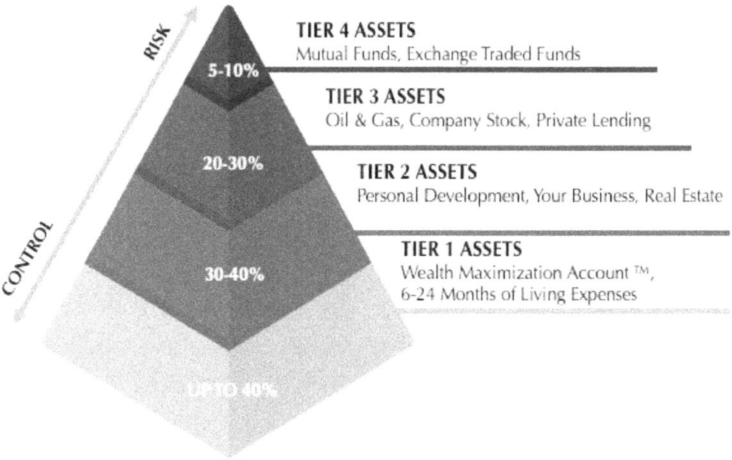

Source: Paradigm Life

Tier 1 (WMA). The base of your pyramid (see above) is where you protect yourself and your family from key risks such as death, disability, and lawsuits. It's also where you store your cash reserves, such as bank accounts, money market accounts, CDs and cash value life insurance. Your WMAguarantees those reserves against loss and makes the money accessible whenever you need it. Tier 1 is the safe and liquid part of your financial life and not the area where you're seeking high returns. A sizable portion of your wealth – say, 40% to 50% – should be here before you begin putting your money at risk.

Tier 2 (Business & Real Estate). Once you establish Tier 1, you work your way up the hierarchy into investments that you can control and influence. These include investments in your professional education, personal developments and networks. Your No. 1 asset is ***you*** and your ability to provide value to the most important people in your life.

Tier 2 can also include assets that grow and create income, such as your own businesses or direct ownership of rental real estate. Both businesses and rental real estate give you greater control than the stock and bond markets do; plus, they throw off growth, income and tax benefits. Many clients keep 30% to 40% of their assets in Tier 2, and you can leverage money from Tier 1 to finance these assets.

Tier 3 (Syndication). Here is where you can take on more risk, such as startup businesses, investments and assets, which have collateral but are controlled by others, including private lending and real estate syndications (e.g., apartment buildings, self-storage, mobile home parks) that are backed by assets. Because there is a degree of risk here, don't allocate more than 10% to 20% of your assets to Tier 3.

Tier 4 (Speculation). Here is where you can take on more risk by investing in assets that you neither control nor influence – assets hat are not backed by collateral. This is where you allocate a smaller portion of your assets (e.g., 5%) to invest in stocks, bonds, mutual funds and even cryptocurrency – since you have the least control and the highest degree of risk in Tier 4.

KEY STEP 2: FOCUS ON WHAT YOU CAN CONTROL

As another old saying goes: "The only thing we can control is our attitude and effort." If you do that, the best possible outcomes will follow.

As we've seen in the very recent past with the pandemic, life can be unpredictable. Life has also become extremely complex, given how connected the globe is currently and the plethora of information at our fingertips. Add to that the external pressures of society that continue to mount and drive us crazy. How best to cope? Focus on what you can control and be prepared for what you cannot.

Plan for the best and prepare for the worst. It can be easy to let our emotions get the best of us...but we can't. Yes, we all are human and will have emotional reactions. In his book *The Obstacle Is the Way/Ego Is the Enemy*, author Ryan Holiday explains: "You can always remind yourself: I am in control, not my emotions. I see what's really going on here. I'm not going to get excited or upset." Reacting puts something or someone else in control, whereas responding gives us the control to dictate what something means and to determine how the outcomes might impact us.

In other words, we can easily let our emotions drive our perception about what is happening to us, and we can create stories to rationalize the situation to ourselves in ways that simply aren't true. For instance, people who aren't happy with the current state of their finances may tell themselves, "I've never been smart about money" or "I can't figure out finances." These emotionally driven cop-outs simply create a false narrative that enables you to keep making costly money mistakes. **STOP!**

Instead of listening to the lies you tell yourself about money, ask yourself two things:

1. "What can I control in my life?"
2. "What is out of my control?"

In her book *Becoming AntiFragile: Learning to Thrive through Disruption, Challenge and Change*, Dr. Paige Williams provides a simple exercise you can use to determine your base of control for a situation. Across the top of a piece a paper, write the following words: **Can't, Can, Influence, Action**. Then put your thoughts down under each word, listing what you clearly can and cannot control, what you can influence, and what actions you can take. By being concrete about these things, you can focus your attention and ultimately your action on things that you are able to impact. Too often we get ourselves worried or upset about things we have little to no control over. It's just not a good use of our energy and brainpower.

FACING OBSTACLES

Obstacles never stop coming. You can hide, or you can deal with them. It's naïve to think that obstacles and challenges will never come your way. They will. They're a given in life, like death and taxes. The challenge is to change your mindset, so you embrace struggle and adversity rather than run from them. After all, struggle and adversity are important parts of life and essential for your growth and success.

For instance, nobody wants to talk about death, but we all know we will die eventually. So, what can we do now to protect our families after we are gone, so they can thrive in the future? After all, you cannot control when you die, but you can control how it impacts your family.

Dr. Williams believes that society has essentially allowed us to be become fragile, as we rely on external factors. She also believes we tend to demonize failure as we seek perfection. According to Dr. Williams, by deploying the right strategies to master our energy (physical, emotional and mental), attitude (confident, constructive and courageous) and mindset (centered on growth and benefiting the world at large), we can become "antifragile." Doing so, says Dr. Williams, will allow us not only to survive during times of massive disruption but to THRIVE.

From where I sit, becoming antifragile allows us to handle disruptions in our lives while also becoming stronger as a result of them. Here are four keys to handling disruption the antifragile way:

- Embrace change rather than resist it.
- Lean into challenge rather than avoid it.
- Learn to thrive when times get tough.
- Learn to become stronger (not angrier or more fearful) as a result of disruption.

As Ryan Holiday would argue, an obstacle is an advantage, not a form of adversity. What he means is that your enemy is not an external force, but rather any mindset that prevents you from seeing things this way.

BEING ACCOUNTABLE

Take personal responsibility, and don't blame others. Yes, there are many things we cannot control (e.g., the weather), but we can take responsibility to prepare for those things (check the forecast, bring along items to deal with the storm, etc.). This requires taking action to learn, discover and change when needed. This will enhance our power and grant us the best chance to achieve our goals.

FINANCIAL FOOTPRINTS

The typical financial advice is centered around some key strategies intended to gain control over our wealth. These are the strategies used by financial institutions so THEY can win even if we don't:

1. **They want us to give them our money.**
2. **They want it consistently on an ongoing basis.**
3. **They want to keep our money for as long as possible.**
4. **They want to give back as little as possible.**

Does this sound familiar?

This keeps most people out of control of their wealth for the bulk of their lives.

The retirement plans developed by most financial advisors are based on assumptions we cannot control (e.g., interest rates, taxes, economic conditions, life expectancy). Yes, it's good to have a plan, but recognize that the plan will change, and you need to be prepared to change in order for it to succeed.

Also, consider where most of people's wealth is invested for retirement: qualified plans (e.g., 401(k), IRAs, SEPs, etc.) that are invested in the stock market. Yes, it's easy and convenient, and it doesn't require people to do too much to manage it. But how much control must you give up? Can you access your money when you want to? What will be the tax rates be in the future when you need the money? How much control do you have over investment performance? Who controls the rules on these types of accounts? There are a host of other areas of our financial worlds that may seem good on the surface but, as you'll see if you dig a bit deeper, may not be in your best interest.

Think about banks for a second. A bank is a place where almost all of our dollars go first. It's also the place where most people store their "safe" dollars so they can access them easily. Yes, banks are convenient, but given the miniscule interest they give you on your money, you are essentially falling behind inflation when you store your money in a bank.

But do you think banks simply sit on those dollars you've given them? Of course, not; they use your money to create ***more money*** for themselves by loaning it out to other people just like you. They are in the business of "marking up" money...your money. Even if you could earn 1% on your checking or savings account, you would not be keeping up with inflation; meanwhile, banks are tripling their return on ***your*** money by loaning it out at 4%.

A different approach to gain more control over your wealth is to follow the Hierarchy of Wealth. As discussed earlier in this chapter, by building the right foundation you can prepare for any obstacle life throws your way with adequate protections and access to available cash – i.e., money that can't be lost. These are foundational pieces that allow you to keep investing with confidence while you withstand any financial torpedoes that come your way.

Most people think achieving their financial and life goals starts with investing. That's what Wall Street wants us to believe. Instead, you should focus on protecting your No. 1 number asset…yourself. You need to create a foundation for your financial and life plan that stays on track even if you are faced with disability, lawsuits or even death.

- The Family Bank strategy can not only provide the best foundational piece for our financial lives (for safety and liquidity), but also create lifelong access to liquidity to fund anything in life AND pass on wealth to the next generation.

We all need to pay for things. Why not explore alternative approaches for building wealth and security that allow you and your family – not the financial institutions that hold your money – to benefit from your assets? This is part of the foundation of the Hierarchy of Wealth. It protects your most valuable asset (by the way, that's you), provides a tremendous tool to store wealth safely and provides a financing arm you control. To learn more, request my Family Bank guide.

- Overall, doing things that can reduce taxes, fees, and other hidden wealth eroders will give you more control over your money so you can deploy it for what you care most about. Everyone wants to keep more of their hard-earned wealth, but the typical advice people get from their financial institutions and advisors – while often sound – is chock full of hidden wealth eroders.
- Protection, savings, liquidity, and reducing wealth eroders are the foundational pieces of everyone's financial life.

My complimentary guide ***Hidden Wealth Eroders*** has more about recapturing the wealth you're losing gradually each and every day.

KEY STEP 3: BE COURAGEOUS

Fear is a powerful thing and can keep many from meeting their full potential in life. It can keep people in a job they dislike. It can prevent people from meeting a person they might have an interest in or from sharing their brilliant ideas. As I mentioned before, external pressures push us to be "right" all the time and to avoid conflict. The reality is that we are perfectly imperfect beings who are meant to learn and grow and fail. It's what we do with that failure that defines what we will become and achieve.

"On the other side of your maximum fear are all the best things in life." – Will Smith

Fear can overwhelm people. It can paralyze them so they're unable to take action. But as FDR told Americans at the start of World War II: "The only thing we need to fear is fear itself." Ask yourself if your greatest fears are real or imaginary. If real, ask yourself what's the worst that can happen if those fears come true. If they do, it's often not as bad as you think. From a perspective of stoicism, you can attack your fears (which are emotionally based) by using logic instead. Don't let FEAR – also an acronym for "false evidence appearing real" – cloud your judgment.

Here are some good ways I've found to take courageous steps:

1. **Don't succumb to the fear of failure.** Think about what success looks like for the next big challenge (or fear) you're facing. What are the steps you need to take, within reason, to get that successful outcome? Athletes, performers and entrepreneurs do this all the time. Why can't you?

   As Oprah Winfrey has asked her legions of followers: "What is the next right move?" By that she means the sooner you figure out what you are supposed to be doing, the sooner you are able to go about the business of doing that. And then you go on to your next right move from there.

   If your goals seem too daunting or too ambitious, you may be tempted to throw in the towel before even trying to reach them. Reaching ambitious goals takes time and dedication. Focusing on one small step at a time is the key to making progress. Isn't that easier than trying to "eat an entire elephant" all at once? Best-selling author Bill Hogan wrote an entire book about this incremental approach: *How Do You Eat an Elephant? One Bite at a Time.*

2. **Take action and do something.** You might fail and be uncomfortable, but the more you do, the easier it gets. Look at each failure as a teaching moment rather than a setback; it gives you insights you can use for the next step in your journey, so you get better and better. Failure is great feedback to let you know you're figuring things out. If you think of it that way, it's all a part of the journey and not a reflection on you and your value to the world.
3. **Don't take yourself too seriously.** Most of us don't like to make fools of ourselves, and we certainly don't want people to ridicule us. When I was younger, I worried constantly about what people thought about me. As a result, I tended to stay silent and kept my ideas to myself. I didn't ask the question or push an idea. I made the situation bigger than it needed to be. Trust me, most people are not thinking about you anyway; they're mainly concerned about themselves and their family. In a situation that you find stressful, step back for a moment to assess the situation for what it truly is. Likely it won't be life-or-death or result in the negative outcomes you may envision. Don't make these moments heavier than they actually are.
4. **Don't have regrets in life.** In his book *The Five Regrets of the Dying*, author Bronnie Ware argues that people's first regret is centered around courage (or lack thereof). She believes you must have the courage to live your best life on your terms, not on the terms you believe others set for you. Many people are afraid to live their lives this way, however, and they ultimately come to regret it.

FINANCIAL FOOTPRINTS

Many people tell themselves they're not good with money or it's too complicated for them to understand. That's just an excuse. While Wall Street relies on quants and advanced technology to compete, the core aspects of your personal finances are not complex. So, a few simple steps can help you gain some additional confidence as you start learning and exposing yourself more to a given area.

Having a strong financial foundation allows you to protect your assets, income and life. Having an estate plan in place will ensure that your wishes for your family and your wealth are completed even if you're not here to see it happen. Building the financial foundation gives you the springboard and confidence to invest for growth. The Family Bank helps provide the protection and capital to do just that.

The Family Bank protects your family from death and disability and has wealth that is growing guaranteed. Having this in place will allow you to venture into investments with courage, as you'll know you can weather any storm that hits.

As mentioned in the description of Tier 2 of the Hierarchy of Wealth, this is where you can start investing in things that you can control and understand. Think investing in real estate or starting your own business. Having deep knowledge and control over your investments reduces your risk and gives you the courage to explore alternatives that may serve you and your family more.

In addition to real estate, there are numerous ways to invest outside of the stock market that may be better suited for you. It just takes courage (and of course some time) to start exploring. You may be shocked to learn what else is available to you. Whether starting a business, investing in your personal development, or trading cryptocurrencies, there are infinite opportunities for those brave enough to try.

By the way, real estate investing is not something that the Dave Ramseys and Suze Ormans of the world will recommend to their millions of Main Street followers. Their advice is fine if you want to master the basics: max out your 401(k), pay your credit cards in full, pay down your mortgage quickly. But if you've read this far in my book, congrats. You and I have something in common: We don't want to be average in any aspect of our lives – including our money. We're looking for ways to accumulate substantial wealth so we can live our best life and pass on what we want to the people and causes that matter most.

Let me ask you this: If conventional wisdom is true, then how come the vast majority of people in this country are not wealthy? To be extraordinary requires that you step away from the herd and separate yourself. Average advice will lead to average results, but I don't think that's what you're seeking. Also, when listening to mainstream advice on a topic, it's important to understand why certain advisors may be recommending their strategy. It might be truthful and objective but understanding how it may benefit them is important to your decision making.

In my case, when I first started learning about real estate investing, it was scary. But I went in with an open mind and just started reading everything I could about the topic. There are some tremendous resources and books out there, such as ***Think Realty***, ***Bigger Pockets***, ***Rich Dad Poor Dad***, ***The ABCs of Real Estate Investing*** and ***Building Wealth One House at a Time***. I also connected with as many real estate experts as I could about using real estate as a foundation for building wealth. I recall my first real estate investing meetup, where I met my first partner. These meetups can be intimidating at first. But the more I pushed myself, the easier it got as my confidence steadily grew. I met a number of tremendous experts. They were very generous with me, and I want to pass that knowledge on to you. There are many ways to invest in real estate, so it's key to be curious and see which options fit you and what you're trying to achieve.

In addition to real estate, starting your own business can be a great way to diversify your income and create an asset that could hugely benefit you and your family for generations to come. For starters, it can be something small in an area where you have some passion and expertise. It all starts with determining what problem you're solving for your customer and how you and/or your service can best address it. Align that with your unique skills and talents, and you have the makings of a business that can impact so many and provide you with wealth you get to control.

KEY STEP 4: BUILD THE RIGHT HABITS

Winning the lottery or experiencing overnight fame and fortune is a wonderful blessing, but for most people success takes time. It requires dedication, persistence and, most important, adopting the right habits and routines on a daily basis. Conversely, adopting the wrong habits can lead us down the wrong path, and once that happens, it can be hard to retrace our steps.

Most successful people have rituals and habits that start the moment they wake up in the morning; that seems like a great place to start. There are a number of versions of a daily routine, but the one that has helped me the most is the SAVERS approach (silence, affirmations, visualizations, exercise, reading, scribe) described in Hal Elrod's *The (6-minute) Miracle Morning*. The idea is to kick-start your day with positivity and empowerment instead of the snooze button or stress.

Creating new habits is not easy; it requires some experimentation and discipline. It can take anywhere from three weeks to nearly an entire year to fully ingrain a new habit. Start small so as not to make it too overwhelming, and ensure the new habits are tied to something you truly want and are motivated to achieve. For instance, if you're looking to drop 20 pounds this year, completely overhauling your diet may be too big a task and thus won't be sustainable but switching out soda for water instead might be a great start. Just like with our finances, small habit changes compounded over time can make a big difference.

Lastly, for building the right habits, I recommend that you tie new habits to an already existing habit. This makes it a little easier to get started, as you have something solid on which to anchor something new.

Many people will tell you they don't have enough time in the day to get everything done. But how do some of the world's most successful - and extremely busy - people do it? Do they have unlimited energy? Do they never sleep? Maybe that's the case for Elon Musk, but in most cases, it's their finely tuned good habits that separate them from the rest of us.

When you think about your daily routine and habits, which aspects of your day are truly helping you reach your goals, and which ones are standing in your way? Taking an inventory of your core habits can help you determine which ones you want to keep and which ones to let go of. Don't be wishy washy here. You have two choices:

1. **If the habit is helping you get closer to your life goals, keep it (and improve it).**
2. **If not, do yourself a favor and drop the habit.**

Author and motivational speaker Darren Hardy's book *The Compound Effect* is a great resource for helping you make big changes in your life with confidence. As people try to make positive new habits stick, they often get frustrated when they don't see immediate results. But it's only after weeks or months of committing to a new habit that you can see tangible results from your commitment to it. At some point, several weeks or months later, you will look back at your former life and be pleasantly surprised to see how far you have come.

MAKE SUNDAY PLANNING A HABIT

One habit I strongly recommend that you develop is Sunday Planning. Starting your week out right means getting your weekly game plan together BEFORE your busy week gets started. One of the best tools I've come across is Hardy's Sunday Planning Worksheet (see below) from. He believes that to get your weekly planning off on the right foot, you need to think very carefully on Sunday (when things are calmer) about your ***key priorities for the week ahead and how those priorities are aligned with your major goals for the year.***

Hardy suggests we focus only on three BIG goals. Remember the earlier exercise in which you set your vision and identified the areas in life you want to impact? During this new exercise, you affirm your BIG Three goals for the year. Then, for the upcoming week, you list your key priorities, projects and tasks that move you forward to reaching those BIG Three goals.

Putting your key items in writing will declutter your mind and prevent you from getting overwhelmed by all the tasks on your to-do list. The Sunday Planning Worksheet also allows you to focus your attention on the most important things so you can get them on your calendar.

Once you've done that, the Miscellaneous section in the lower-right quadrant of the worksheet gives you space to add additional initiatives you could tackle **AFTER** your key priority items for the week are addressed. Having them on paper will free your mind from worrying about them.

Finally, the most important part of Sunday Planning is determining which of your three priorities is most important. This is likely the bigger project, initiative, etc. that commands more of your time and is essential to moving you closer to your goals. If nothing else gets done, you want to make sure your highest-priority items within that top goal are addressed in the week ahead.

In Chapter 3, we'll talk more about integrating Sunday Planning with your other time management techniques.

Source: Darren Hardy

FINANCIAL FOOTPRINTS

Saving is the foundation of a good financial plan at any age, in any economic climate. But with interest rates so low recently (i.e., penalizing savers), saving has become a lost art. Additionally, saving has been commingled with investing, which it shouldn't be. As PEM founder Kim Butler often says: "Saving saves lives." This should be one of the core habits in your financial life.

To clarify, your savings comprise money that you're accumulating that only goes in one direction...up. There is little risk of your principal being lost. And you easily have access to the funds whenever you need them. Most people think simply plunking money into a 401(k) is a form of saving, but retirement accounts are actually "risk assets," since the value of the account can fluctuate with the financial markets, and you can't access that money without penalty until age 59½.

Again, investing is using money that you're trying to grow – but of course, that comes with risk of loss. You need low-risk liquid savings to stock your emergency cash fund (six to 12 months of basic living expenses). In addition to your emergency cash, you need extra liquid savings to take advantage of business or investment opportunities that come your way unexpectedly. For many people, the only thing worse than losing money is not having enough liquid cash to take advantage of a great opportunity.

You also need liquid savings to finance the down payment on a new home or to pay for college. If you think you'll be needing to tap your money sooner, do you want to put it at risk and possibly not have enough? Also, if you don't have savings available and something happens, you may have to liquidate your investments, with potential penalties or tax consequences. You might also need to utilize expensive debt, such as by borrowing on a credit card, which can reach very high rates.

All too often, even well-educated, financially savvy professionals can find themselves short on liquid cash when the unexpected in life comes their way.

My point is that even if you're a good saver, just socking your money away in a "savings account," even if it's considered "high yield," won't do much for you in today's extremely low interest rate environment. You need a better place to save your money that is liquid, so it earns a decent return, can't be lost, and is protected from tax and creditors. This is where the Family Bank strategy comes into play. It's a powerful way to store your wealth efficiently while also allowing you to use your money for investment purposes – to grow your wealth while protecting your family from the consequences of your death or disability.

In addition to the foundation of savings, it is key that you evaluate your financial reality periodically (annually at least) to ensure that your financial world is evolving with you, your life and your priorities. Remember, money is just the tool to serve what you want in life, and it's up to you to take the reins to ensure it's working as hard as possible for you. Whether you do it yourself or secure advisors to help you, it's crucial to evaluate what you're doing in the key areas of your financial life: Protection, Savings, Growth, Debt and Cash Flow. Maintaining an efficient model will enable to you keep more of your money and put it to its best possible use for you and your family. By not doing that, you're leaving it for others to leverage and benefit from.

KEY LEARNINGS FROM CHAPTER 1:

- Working just to make money – no matter how well you're compensated – will never provide you with satisfaction or bring you closer to your family. I learned this the hard way.
- You need to clarify your vision for your ideal future. The R-Factor Question can help.
- After framing your ideal future, assess where you are in the

key areas of life (business, financial, physical, mental, family, spiritual, lifestyle, relationships). The Life Assessment grid in this chapter can help.

- If certain key areas of your life are not in alignment with your goals and values, you're not alone. Pick three areas of your life you most want to improve and, for each, ask yourself: (a) "Who do I want to become?" (b) "What do I want to achieve?" and (c) "What things must I stop doing, and what things should I start doing?"
- The LEAP Model (*Lifetime Economic Acceleration Process*™) provides a good framework for looking at your entire financial life from five unique viewpoints (Protection, Savings, Growth, Debt and Cash Flow).
- The Hierarchy of Wealth is a proven way to build wealth without exposing yourself to excessive risk, and to gain more control over your money than you have with qualified retirement plans and stock market investments.

Please review the Key Learnings above before moving on to Chapter 2.

CHAPTER TWO

Build Self-Awareness And Create Your Unique Impact

"I alone cannot change the world, but I can cast a stone across the waters to create many ripples."

- Mother Theresa

Throughout my life I've focused on external, rather than internal, factors for clues about what defines success. While I never felt I was the smartest guy in the room, I usually feel like I'm among the hardest working. Most people think I have a lot of energy, but until recently, I never focused my energy on one of the most important areas of life – myself. More specifically, I never worked on my self-awareness – learning more about myself and what motivates me and gives me a sense of fulfillment. I'm sure many of you can relate to that.

By the way, focusing on self-awareness does not make you selfish. It makes you smart and will help you get more out of your relationships with the people you care about most. When you feel fulfilled and abundant, you'll have more to share with others.

Sure, I had some clues to my psyche early on. For instance, I excelled at sports in my younger days and always liked to compete. But I didn't understand what my true gifts were or what my purpose was in life. Those questions were too big for me to ponder in my teens and early adult life, and I wasn't ready to face them.

"The two most important days in your life are the day you are born and the day you find out why." - Mark Twain

KEY STEP 5: DISCOVER YOURSELF

Countless studies have shown that to be truly happy and live your best life, you must know deep down what brings you satisfaction and fulfillment. You must be crystal clear about what motivates you to get out of bed early on cold, dark winter mornings to do the things you know in your gut you need to accomplish each day. You also need to be clear about the things that repel you, demotivate you, frustrate you and anger you – the barriers to your growth and progress.

I know many people aren't comfortable digging deep into their psyche, but it's an essential part of growing and gaining self-awareness. American society doesn't encourage us to explore self-awareness because it doesn't define success on those terms. No, we're encouraged to seek wealth and fame – NOT balance and self-fulfillment.

Think about all the athletes, celebrities, and business tycoons who seem to have it all: money, fame, power, etc. But if you spent any time with them, you'd often see deep down they don't feel happy or fulfilled.

Once you discover your inner passions and motivations, you'll have a gold mind of information to pave your path forward.

WHAT DO YOU VALUE?
WHAT'S YOUR PURPOSE AND MISSION IN LIFE?

These are big, weighty questions that can take lots of time and self-reflection to answer. Don't rush it.

Simon Sinek's best seller *Start with Why* can be a great resource for crystallizing your purpose. It provides an easy yet powerful way to change your mindset.

As mentioned earlier, self-awareness is a very powerful attribute that many of us don't acquire until we've gained maturity and life experiences. Taking stock of what you truly value will help you determine if you're living a life that's in alignment with what you value. I realize the path to self-awareness is not easy. Just know you don't need to go it alone.

Consider hiring a coach (as discussed earlier, in the section on leveraging experts) to help you. The *Blueprint Process* can be great resource. Or you can take it upon yourself to assess what makes you unique. Use the tools below to help you understand what makes you tick and what drives your thoughts, beliefs, and actions, and how your values show up in your day-to-day life.

List 5-10 of your most important values below.

Need help with your values list? Here are some resources to help you get started:

- Brene Brown's "*Dare to Lead*" list of personal values.
- *The World's Most Influential Values* (Visual Capitalist)

I realize coming up with this list can be hard. For starters, consider the people you admire the most. What draws you to them? This can be a clue to what you truly value. Next, organize your values into categories that make sense to you, such as "Personal Growth" or "Learning" or "Service," and then select your core values from the remining list. There is no magic number, but a list of 5-10 values is a good target.

As part of your self-awareness journey, you may find it interesting to see *which values are universally important* no matter which country or part of the world you're from.

Now that you've come up with your most important core values, review your list one more time, and make sure those values align with how you are living your life. That can include the work you do; your relationships with friends, colleagues and family; and how you interact with your community and your faith.

DETERMINING YOUR UNIQUE SKILLS, TALENTS, AND PASSIONS

I've always been a very curious person. When I get interested in a topic, I tend to immerse myself in it and try to learn everything I can about it from every possible angle. Sometimes I go down rabbit holes and take endless detours in my search for knowledge, and before I know it, hours and hours have passed. I know we hate "wasting" time in our time-obsessed society, but when you get so fascinated with a certain topic that you lose all track of time when pursuing it, that's a pretty good clue it's one of your passions – something that gives you boundless energy to push forward on the trail of knowledge.

Conventional wisdom tells us that if you do what you love for a living, you'll never "work" a day in your life. Unfortunately, many hardworking people are just "grinding it out," trying to make it to the weekend. They have no idea what their passions are. My take is that you need to explore your passions and tie them into your purpose on this earth.

To identify your passions, think about the things that bring you positive energy when you're engaged in them instead of taking your energy away. It could be a highly rewarding project at your job or a hobby you can't wait to get back to. These activities are clues to your true passions. When you're engaged in these activities that bring you positive energy, you lean into them, learn as much as you can about them, and feel good about yourself while immersed in them. The more you engage, the more you develop a passion and know it's something you can pursue for the rest of your life.

For some people it's surfing, skiing, woodworking, or playing chess. For me, it's personal finance and learning everything I can about the topic so I can help others. It took me a while to realize this, but now I know it's one of my passions and something I can devote the rest of my life to pursuing and mastering.

IDENTIFYING YOUR STRENGTHS

Do you know what your biggest strengths are and how they show up in your daily living? Leveraging your core strengths will allow you to unearth your greatest contribution to the world and help other people understand what makes you truly unique. As for many of you, the mentors in my life – my parents, teachers, coaches, bosses, etc. – advised me to shore up my weaknesses. I was more of an introvert and would prefer not to engage in social situations or take the lead. I've grown quite a bit more confident in this area, but I'll certainly never be mistaken for an extrovert or a natural schmoozer. Sure, there's some merit to improving your weaknesses, but I know I can make a much greater contribution to the world by leveraging my strengths. We all have strengths – they are our superpowers. Ask yourself: "What can I be world-class at?" And then surround yourself with others who can balance your deficiencies.

I was never the best communicator or writer during my academic career. It's amazing to think I'm actually writing a book now. However, thanks to my growth mindset, I know that I can improve my written and communication skills – skills I never thought would be worth developing. You need to figure what skills are most important for your success and determine if you want to develop them or potentially leverage others who have found them to be their gift.

Still not sure what your true inner strengths are? The *Clifton Strengths Assessment* is another good tool for *measuring your talents* based on your natural patterns of thinking, feeling and behaving. Among other things, the CliftonStrengths Assessment will help you:

- Discover what you naturally do best.
- Learn how to develop your greatest talents into strengths.
- Use your personalized results and reports to maximize your potential.

The *KOLBE Index* is another powerful tool that helps identify the ways you tend to take action when you strive. Your result will tell you more about your natural strengths and the unique way you solve problems. Many companies use the KOLBE Index to align their core values with how people use their greatest gifts to attack problems and perform tasks. By understanding how you prefer to solve problems, you can gain insight into how to balance your work team to optimize outcomes and decision-making.

One of the greatest benefits of strength assessment tests is they help you recognize how you can contribute to the world in your own unique way – and achieve even greater heights via collaboration. Knowing that you don't have to do it all or do it alone should give you the courage and confidence to pursue your dreams.

FINANCIAL FOOTPRINTS

How would you respond if asked what your most valuable financial asset is? Some might say their home. Others would say their retirement accounts. However, the fact is that ***you*** are your No. 1 financial asset, because only you can create value for others through your unique work and business. Author Robert Kiyosaki defines an asset as anything that puts money in your pocket. So, wouldn't you agree that you are your No. 1 asset?

If you are your biggest asset, wouldn't it be wise to protect yourself to the max? True, most people don't do so because of the perceived high cost of insurance and other wealth protection solutions. But the cost of not doing so can be enormous if something unfortunate were to happen to you.

In addition to protecting your best asset, you can increase the value of that asset. This is where Tier 2 of the Hierarchy of Wealth comes into play (see Chapter 1). It's all about investing in your personal development. Whether working a job or running a business, investing in your professional development can generate massive returns on that investment. How? Because you are now able to bring more value to your employer (and get compensated for it) or grow your business under your leadership and control. It's likely the best return you can get from an investment.

Legendary author and motivational speaker Zig Ziglar liked to say: ***"You can get everything in life you want if you will just help enough other people get what they want."***

People often ask me: "Where should I invest?" There's no one-size-fits-all answer to that question, because so much depends on your goals, your risk tolerance, and where you are in your financial life.

There's much more to it than finding investments with the highest returns. It's really more about identifying your goals, risk tolerance, and stage of life, and then finding investments that best fit with those needs.

As you explore different investments, you'll want to be able to answer two key questions before you put down your hard-earned money: (1) **What's the purpose of the investment?** and (2) **What's your level of interest, expertise and experience in the investment?** Let's take a closer look at each:

1. What's the purpose of the investment? We can get so wrapped up in the "shiny object syndrome," or the next hot stock touted on TV and radio investment shows, that we forget to consider how that investment fits into our own unique financial situation. What's appropriate for the masses may not be appropriate for you and your family – and vice versa.

Are you looking to increase passive income to support your lifestyle or replace your job? Are you looking to help fund a future purchase (e.g., a vacation house), or will it be used someday to help fund life after your current employment? Understanding where any investment aligns with your unique financial goals is absolutely critical. ***Money without purpose is poverty.***

2. What's your level of interest, expertise and experience in the investment? I've mentioned that having direct control of your investment (e.g., real estate, business) will greatly reduce your risk of loss. You can also reduce your investment by putting money into businesses or industries in which you have a lot of personal experience. I realize this can take additional time and effort, but isn't it worth it to protect and grow the wealth you worked so hard to create?

Remember the pyramid (Hierarchy of Wealth) back in Chapter 1: you want to invest in things that you find interesting and have some control over. It could be owning a piece of property that you rent out for income or starting a business for which you're the primary owner and hence in control of the business's future.

DON'T CHASE MONEY

Volumes have been written about the axiom "***Don't chase the money.***" In other words, you should never spend all of your time and effort working just to accumulate more money. I've heard countless stories and experienced it firsthand: if money is the sole object you're chasing, you could be chasing it forever with no increase in satisfaction. There's a saying that money is the root of all evil. I don't think that's correct; it's the LOVE of money that is root of all evil. Instead of focusing on money, focus on serving your family, customers, clients, patients, etc. to the absolute best of your abilities, and the money will naturally follow.

It's easy to get consumed by chasing wealth, and that often means deferring enjoyment of life, if not outright missing out. Instead, focus on ways to bring more value to your work, your business, and your investing. Doing so will increase your chances of having more wealth come your way.

Oprah Winfrey is fond of repeating a favorite quote from Martin Luther King, Jr.: "***Greatness is determined by service.***" Like King, Oprah believes everyone can be great at something if they bring significance and value to what they do for others. What Oprah is trying to convey is that the more value you bring to others, the greater the chance you will be rewarded financially. In other words, the wealth you accumulate is not the end goal. Instead, wealth is the result of the great work and service you provide.

One of my clients had a successful career in corporate America for over 30 years and retired early to pursue his passion – teaching and inspiring others how to innovate. So, he started his own firm that helps business professionals become more creative in their work so they can achieve more success and fulfillment. Through his journey, he has grown more passionate about his cause, and he is enjoying a freedom of life and business he hadn't experienced before.

Yes, it's important to ensure you are personally taken care of. You need money to live and to support the people and causes that matter most to you. To paraphrase Oprah, you still need to "fill your cup each day" and feel personally empowered so you can empower others to live their best lives. I have always found that when your proverbial cup is full, it's easy to share your talents, skills, and expertise with others and to provide them with exceptional value and service.

See Oprah's iconic *commencement speech video* for more. You might also enjoy the epic *2018 Super Bowl victory speech* from Philadelphia Eagles center Jason Kelce. ***WARNING: Kelce's language is a little rough around the edges, but his passion for the cause is second to none.***

KEY STEP 6: ADOPT THE RIGHT MINDSET

In addition to having the right habits in place, fostering the right mindset for success can give you the support you need in challenging times. Your mindset is the set of beliefs that you have on how the world works, and that direct how you think, act and behave.

- Do you believe people are inherently good or evil?
- Do you believe intelligence is fixed or developable?
- Do you believe conflict is positive or negative?
- Do you believe that a rising tide lifts all boats, or that for one person to win another has to lose?

These are just some basic questions that can help uncover what may be driving your behaviors and priorities.

ESTABLISH AN ABUNDANCE MINDSET, AND BE READY FOR OPPORTUNITIES

The concept of an "abundance" mindset was developed by author Stephen Covey in his 1989 best seller, *The Seven Habits of Highly Effective People*. While volumes have been written about abundance since then, Covey simply defined it as a mindset in which a person believes there are "enough resources and successes to share with others."

That's a big difference from what he called the "scarcity" mindset, which is based on the idea that life is a zero-sum game – if someone else wins or is successful in a situation, which means you lose.

Certified coach and yoga luminary Nicolette Stinson offers *10 steps for developing an "abundance mindset"*:

1. **Recognize the Power of Your Thoughts**
2. **Practice Gratitude**
3. **Believe the Sky's the Limit**
4. **Cultivate and Share Your Passions and Purpose**
5. **Develop Mastery Experiences**
6. **Pick Your Words Wisely**
7. **Build Beyond a Growth Mindset**
8. **Think Like a Beginner**
9. **Notice the Good!**
10. **Speak Daily Abundance Affirmations**

Here are three from that list that especially hit home for me:

Cultivate and Share Your Passions and Purpose (Stinson Step 4)

Confucius liked to say: "Choose a job you love, and you'll never have to work a day in your life." However, many people never find their true calling in life and why they exist on this earth. For most people, finding their true passions takes some work; they need to find a way to make a living that keeps them energized, fulfilled and motivated to serve others.

ACTION: Once you build the knowledge and expertise, don't be shy about sharing that passion with the rest of the world. Many other people can benefit from your wisdom.

Build Beyond a Growth Mindset (Stinson Step 7)

Here, Stinson is urging us to get out of the narrow mindset that we're only good at certain things and that we are incapable of developing additional skills and talents. Yes, we have innate strengths, and we should be deliberate about developing and honing them. But a growth mindset comes with the belief that we can learn anything if we put our efforts behind it.

One of the most rewarding parts of life is constantly growing and becoming better each day. This is achieved by staying curious and humble and knowing that we can learn just about anything we set our mind to. Even if we live to be 200 years old, we will never learn it all – but it might be fun trying.

ACTION: Be curious about other people and their experiences. Every day, ask someone about their life, what their goals are and how they plan to achieve those goals. Instead of just setting performance goals, set learning goals to develop new skills and talents.

Notice the Good! (Stinson Step 9)

Humans have a tendency to notice the negative things in life more than they notice the positives. It's simply how our brains have been wired for thousands of years as a means of survival. Ancestors who were quick to detect and react to threats were more likely to stay alive and *pass along their DNA*.

However, in the modern world, many of the life-threatening risks humans once faced are no longer present. Therefore, it's important to see (and appreciate) the good things in life. This optimistic approach to life will make you feel happier and more fulfilled – and will contribute to your longevity.

We'll discuss this in more detail in Chapter 4.

ACTION: The next time you have a perceived problem or challenge, look at it from a more holistic perspective. Instead of focusing on what is going wrong and trying to fix the problem, focus on what is actually going right as it relates to the topic, and brainstorm ways to support that even further.

IMPACT
LOW

THE HAPPINESS ADVANTAGE

How a Positive Brain Fuels Success in Work and Life

The International Bestseller That Has Changed Millions of Lives

SHAWN ACHOR

New York Times Bestselling Author

In his best seller *The Happiness Advantage* (2010), author and motivational speaker Shawn Achor explains how rewiring our brain for happiness helps us achieve more in our careers and our relationships and as students, leaders and parents.

Achor's work resonates with me and with many of our firm's clients because he challenges the conventional wisdom that says you will become successful if you work hard, and that once you become successful, you will be happy. As most of you know, success does NOT automatically translate into happiness – and sometimes it's the reverse. According to Achor, happiness fuels success and performance, not the other way around. Why? Because when we are happier and more positive, we are more engaged, creative, resilient to stress and productive.

Here are several suggestions from Achor about ways to become happier:

- **Gratitude exercises.** Write down three things you're grateful for that occurred over the past 24 hours. They don't have to be profound. It could be a really good cup of coffee or the warmth of a sunny day.
- **Meditation.** Every day, take two minutes to stop whatever you're doing and concentrate on breathing. Even a short mindful break can result in a calmer, happier you.
- **Conscious act of kindness.** At the start of every day, send a short email or text praising someone you know. Our brains become addicted to feeling good by making others feel good.
- **Deepen social connections.** Spend time with family and friends. Our social connections are one of the best predictors of success and health, and even life expectancy.

Related to abundance and positivity, most people are striving for happiness in life. For many, happiness is at the end of the journey to success; it's the outcome they obtain from all their efforts. But what if it worked the other way? What if being happy actually *LEADS* to your success?

FINANCIAL FOOTPRINTS

If we wish to create wealth, we must first examine our thoughts and beliefs. We do this because our consciousness guides our behavior...and our results!

Are we thinking abundantly, or living our lives from the assumptions of scarcity? For instance, if we believe there is "never enough," we could find ourselves compulsively spending every penny we make (and then some). Our thoughts will literally become our reality! And if we believe there is more than enough, we'll find ways to save, to give and to invest in ourselves.

Conversely, scarcity thinking may cause people to hoard money, but not use it, fearing there may NOT be "more where that came from" after all. Some people have been so convinced that there is "never enough" that they hide many thousands of dollars of cash around their house, or even uncashed checks, which are only found later by surprised heirs who believed their dearly departed aunt was poor!

Here are a few habits of prosperous people (possessing the abundance mindset), in contrast to those with a scarcity mindset:

- Prosperous people save what they can rather than spend all they can.
- Prosperous people put their money to use instead of hoarding it.

- Prosperous people focus on giving first rather than getting.
- Prosperous thinking is contribution-based rather than greed-based.
- A prosperous mindset recognizes our limitless value, while scarcity thinking equates security with paychecks, retirement accounts or homes.

EXPAND YOUR PERSPECTIVE: THREE SIDES OF A COIN

Ask most people to examine a coin, and they'll tell you they see two sides: heads and tails. But business legend Robert Kiyosaki (*Rich Dad Poor Dad*) believes there are actually three sides of a coin – the head, the tail and ***the edge***. He believes your ability to understand contrasting points of view and your ability to glean what information you believe to be valuable from each side is a crucial skill. I like to take it a step further: looking at things from the edge in addition to the sides will ensure you make the best possible decision.

The world of personal finance can seem daunting. Many people rely on their investment advisor or CPA to guide them on their financial journey. As you accumulate more assets and more complexity in your life, you'll need to start thinking of your personal finances as a business with you as the CEO and your most trusted financial advisor as your CFO. But that's not the end of it. Think about other experts you need to flesh out your board of advisors. This will ensure that the business of your personal finances is operating as efficiently and effectively as it can.

When seeking out advisors, here are some items to consider:

1. What areas of your financial life do you need help with?
2. What are the advisor's values, and how do they operate their practice?

3. What are the principles and philosophies that drive their opinions on the optimal financial strategies?
4. To what extent do they follow the advice they share with their clients?
5. What are their expectations on how you'll work together?
6. What's the process and approach they use with their clients?

Since this is an extremely important relationship you're building, you want to find an experienced and technically competent advisor – and also one who shares your values.

KEY STEP 7: BALANCE SHORT-TERM THINKING WITH LONG-TERM THINKING

The idea here is to plan for the long term but act in the short term.

Take your health, for example. If you have a desire to be here on earth for a long time, you have to make sure you eat right, exercise daily, reduce stress, quit smoking and keep your consumption of alcohol reasonable. While you might not notice the benefits of these healthy daily habits in the short term, they can have a massive positive impact in the long term. Same goes for your finances. How can you build the right financial habits so that you have the greatest likelihood of long-term financial success? Building the right foundation is key.

PATIENCE AND PERSISTENCE TRUMP OVERNIGHT SUCCESS EVERY TIME

"If you really look closely, most overnight successes took a long time." – Steve Jobs

Whether it's Colonel Sanders, Ray Kroc, Oprah Winfrey, Bill Gates, Steve Jobs, J.K. Rowling, or any other person who has achieved great success, many had to go through substantial trial and error, failure, and disappointment before hitting it big.

But in today's tech-driven world of instant gratification, patience is not a virtue that many possess. Whether it's same-day shipping or quick ways to make a buck through day trading or crypto investing, we've become a society that wants what we want, when we want it, how we want it. However, a lot of success comes from trial and error, hard work, learning, and adapting. This requires discipline, as success in the real world usually does not come right away. It requires failing time and time again until you find the right path.

Case in point: It took Thomas Edison 10,000 attempts to get his revolutionary light bulb to work. Edison never believed he had 9,999 failures. Edison simply said: ***"I have not failed. I have just found 9,999 ways that do not work."***

I'm not sure how many people have Edison's "stick-to-itiveness" today. What I have found over my career is that most people overestimate what they can achieve in one year and underestimate what they can achieve in five years.

Whether it's changing your diet, adopting an exercise, or savings regimen or improving your relationship with your family, it all starts with smaller habits that will compound over time. As mentioned in Chapter 1, Darren Hardy's *The Compound Effect* is a great resource to help you build momentum when it comes to making big changes in your life. You need to be patient and consistent.

One place to start is to figure out what you want to "give up" to make room for more positive disciplines and activities that get you closer to where you want to be. It's just as important to be clear on what you DON'T do, so you can have the time and energy to focus on what you MUST do to become the person you want to be and accomplish your goals.

FINANCIAL FOOTPRINTS

If someone offered you the choice between having $1 million cash today or starting with a penny and having the value double every day for the next 30 days, which one would you choose? Most people tell me they'd rather have the guaranteed $1 million cash in hand. But if you do the math, you'll see starting with a penny and allowing your total to double every day for 30 consecutive days would give you over $5.3 million at the end of that month. That's the power of compounding at work!

To achieve wealth, many people keep buying lottery tickets or investing in crypto and collectibles or speculating in real estate. But success in life – including your finances – comes from slow and steady growth. That takes patience and discipline, which is not easy to accomplish in our fast-paced, instant-gratification society. From consistent saving to growing a business, building wealth takes time. It's almost impossible to get rich quick – and stay rich.

But here's the good news: once your wealth train gets rolling, it picks up momentum with every passing year thanks to the power of compounding.

Now that you understand the basic power of compounding, it's important to understand the different ***phases*** of the compound interest curve. In the example below, if you invested $10,000 per year in the same account for 30 years and stayed fully invested – and earned 7% on that money every year – you would have accumulated over $1 million in 30 years' time. ***That's $300,000 in total capital put in over 30 years + over $700,000 in gains you made on that original $300,000. Not a bad reward for your patience, is it?***

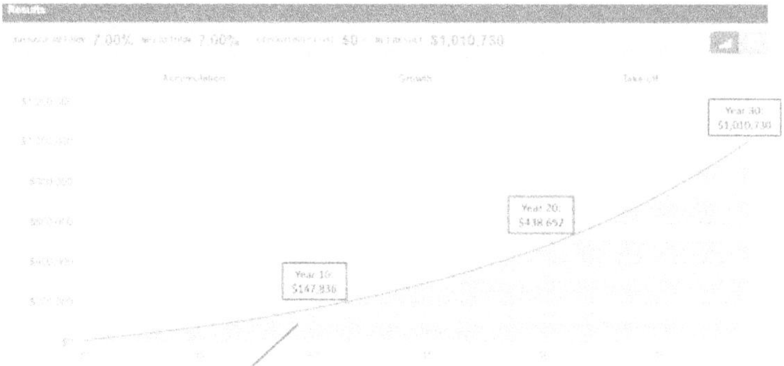

Source: LEAP Systems

Phase 1 (Accumulation): In this phase, your money starts to earn some interest and reaches a modest $148,000 with a total $100,000 contribution through the first 10 years. Not bad, but we're just getting started.

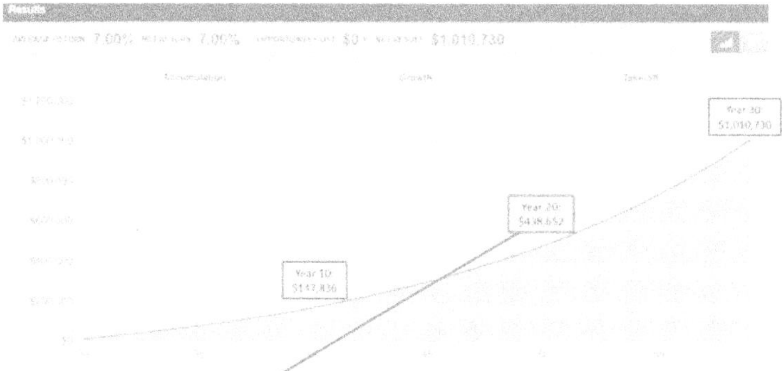

Source: LEAP Systems

Phase 2 (Growth): During the next 10 years, you'll experience some growth in your wealth as your account reaches $439,000. In this phase, the balance of your account grows by more than double what you contributed ($200,000 in growth for $100,000 contributed during the middle 10 years of the curve).

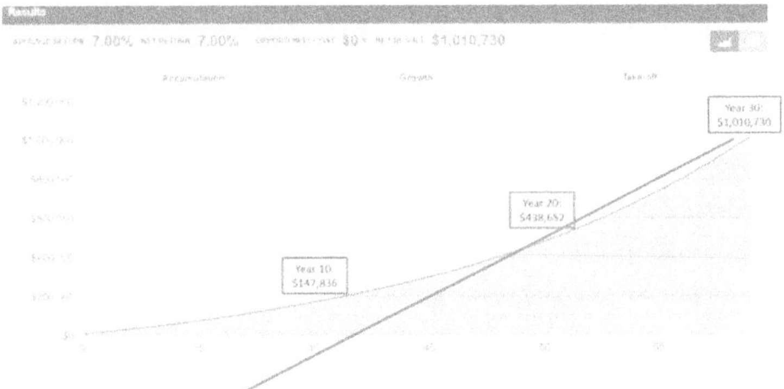

Source: LEAP Systems

Phase 3 (Takeoff): In the final 10 years of this example, we start to see the impact of the interest compounding from the prior 20 years. At this phase, the account balance grows significantly to over $1 million. During this 10-year period, $100,000 in new contributions grows to over $472,000! The consistent approach to saving and investing is really starting to work. Nearly 70% of the gains over the 30-year period in this example occur in this final 10-year phase of the compound interest curve.

Getting there is the hard part. But if you have the patience to do so, the rewards are immense.

Now, take a closer look at the compound interest curve. If you get a late start on your wealth-building years, or if you disrupt the growth with unplanned withdrawals from your account, you delay the steepest part of the growth curve when the greatest appreciation happens.

Whether you spend your money directly or allow it to lose value by paying too much in taxes, fees or depreciation, you're minimizing the amount of wealth you're making available to compound over time. Doing so is a huge Opportunity Cost (***we'll talk more about this in Chapter 3***) that will significantly impact the amount of money you'll have at the end of those 30 years.

For example, suppose you're forced to pay a 1% fee for one of your investments. That doesn't sound too bad, but over 30 years, that 1% annual fee eats up ***$183,514*** of lost compounding, which reduces your gain by more than ***25%***. As you can see, compounding is a great ally when you're an investor and saver, but a real enemy when you're a debtor. Unnecessary fees are just one of many hidden wealth eroders. Add investment losses, heavy spending and taxes, and the erosion of your wealth is significant.

You only have one compound interest curve in your lifetime. Use it wisely. Start saving and investing as early as you can.

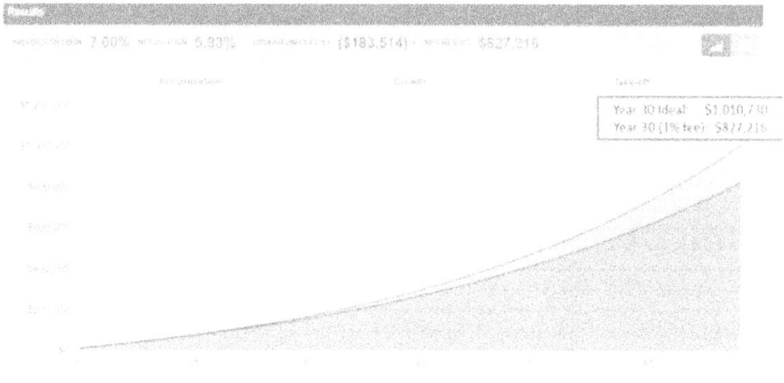

Source: LEAP Systems

Now that you've got a handle on compound interest, let's look at how we finance everything in our lives. As mentioned earlier, Nelson Nash (*Becoming Your Own Banker*) believes we finance everything we buy in one of two ways:

1. We take on debt and pay back principal (with interest).
2. We pay cash and avoid the interest payments.

By taking on debt, you incur substantial interest costs to finance the things you buy. In theory, this frees up cash when you pay for things over time, but in reality, you're simply enriching the lender. For many families, the interest they pay to finance their lifestyle can amount to nearly one-third of their income. ***Talk about a hidden wealth eroder!***

The second approach – paying cash for everything – sounds admirable on the surface. You don't incur any debt (i.e., interest) directly, and you have a clean personal balance sheet. Unfortunately, by tying up all your cash to finance your purchases, you have the Opportunity Cost of not having your money available to keep growing and compounding. To take advantage of the compound interest curve, you want as much of your money as possible to grow uninterrupted – for as long as possible.

So, how can you avoid interest and debt when you don't pay cash for everything you buy? Sounds impossible, but it's not.

FAMILY BANK: THE THIRD OPTION

With a ***Family Bank***, your money compounds uninterrupted in a safe vehicle over a long period of time. Even better, your money can serve as collateral, which enables you to borrow from a mainstream financial institution. Imagine a situation in which your money continually earns compound interest while you leverage someone else's money to finance your life and boost your investments. I know it may sound too good to be true, but it's not.

A Family Bank is a vehicle that allows your family – not an outside financial institution – to control the financing and lending (i.e., banking) functions of everything important in your life. And you don't need to be a Rockefeller, Vanderbilt or Gates to set one up. A Family Bank can work for anyone who can think long term, has disciplined money habits and is open-minded. Even if you're just getting your career or business started, there are opportunities to begin building this key foundational piece of a successful financial life and growing it as your career and cash flow grow. But again, you have to be patient. If you're looking for a get-rich-quick scheme, a Family Bank is not for you.

For more information about this concept, download my free guide ***The Family Bank: A Foundation for Taking Control of Your Financial Future***. The idea is to get as much of your money as possible working and compounding for you for a very long period of time.

KEY STEP 8: BEGIN WITH THE END IN MIND

Most of you are familiar with the Nobel prizes for outstanding achievement in physics, chemistry, physiology, medicine, and literature. But you may not know it was a case of mistaken identity that caused Nobel founder Alfred Nobel, a French explosives tycoon, to create them in 1895.

Nobel never spoke publicly about his motivation for the awards, but many believe it was inspired by an earlier case of mistaken identity. In 1888, Nobel's brother, Ludvig, died in France from a heart attack. Because the media was not as transparent as it is today, at least one French newspaper believed that it was Alfred Nobel who had perished, not his brother, and published a scathing obituary, calling Nobel a "merchant of death" (among other things) who had grown rich by developing new ways to "mutilate and kill."

While the paper later corrected its error, Alfred was already shocked to his core after reading his own death notice and discovering how his legacy would be remembered. According to biographer Kenne Fant, Nobel became "so obsessed with his posthumous reputation that he rewrote his last will, bequeathing most of his fortune to a cause upon which no future obituary writer would be able to cast aspersions." How would you want to be remembered by those you care most about?

As mentioned in Chapter 1, Bronnie Ware (*The Top Five Regrets of the Dying*) asks readers: "What can you start doing now so you don't have any regrets at the end?" Ware believes you have the opportunity right now to embody the wisdom that many realized far too late:

1. "I wish I'd had the courage to live a life true to myself, not the life others expected of me."
2. "I wish I hadn't worked so hard."
3. "I wish I'd had the courage to express my feelings."
4. "I wish I had stayed in touch with my friends."
5. "I wish I had let myself be happier."

If you don't want regrets in life like those described by Ware above, I suggest you ask yourself ASAP what you can start doing to prevent them. It could be as simple as telling your family members that you love them, calling a friend to let them know you're thinking about them or making sure you use your vacation time – all of it. Whatever you choose to do, start today, as you never know when the clock will run out on your game of life. Instead of regrets, wouldn't you rather be able to say, "I lived my life to the fullest, gave my all and left it on the field?" Now that's living!

WHAT LEGACY DO YOU WANT TO LEAVE BEHIND FOR YOUR FAMILY AND OTHER PEOPLE YOU'VE IMPACTED?

Not to be morbid but think about how people would remember you if you passed away suddenly. What would they say, for better or worse? If you don't like your imaginary eulogy and obituary, start trying to become the person you'd want to be remembered as. Richard Branson, Virgin Group founder, believes the character of your children has a bigger impact in terms of the legacy you leave than the wealth you've created or the businesses you've built. That's where a Family Mission Statement (see below) can be very helpful.

"Those who know me know I'm passionate about lists, and top of my list of priorities is my family. My wife Joan and I do not consider our legacy to our children to be wealth or fame but the opportunity to pursue happiness by following their own path."
– Sir Richard Branson

FAMILY MISSION STATEMENT

A Family Mission Statement is a combined, unified expression from all family members of what your family is all about – and the principles by which you choose to govern your family life. If you don't have a Family Mission Statement, let these questions guide you:

1. What is the purpose of our family?

____

____

____

____

2. What do we want to be remembered for?

____

____

____

3. What kind of family do we want to be?

____

____

____

4. What are our responsibilities as family members?

____

____

____

5. What families inspire us, and why do we admire them?

____

____

____

Ask yourself what you want others to say about you at your funeral. As mortals, we eventually will leave this earth, so it's important to start living your life the way you want to be remembered. What do you want your kids and spouse to feel about how you lived your life? How can you start living your life now, so those desires come true?

FINANCIAL FOOTPRINTS

No one likes contemplating their own mortality, but as humans, we must eventually leave this earth. We never know when our time will come, but by planning ahead and putting the right plans in place, we can ensure that our wishes for our money and our legacy are carried out correctly when we have passed on.

1. Create your estate plan and review it regularly

- No one enjoys planning for their departure from earth, but you owe it to your family to have an up-to-date will and estate plan.
- If nothing else, make sure your assets are properly titled and you are crystal clear about your financial and healthcare powers of attorney and about guardians for your minor children.
- Don't make the mistake of thinking that you're not wealthy enough for estate planning – or that your family will never argue about money when you're gone.

"In this world, nothing is certain except death and taxes."
– Benjamin Franklin

It's hard to believe, but studies show *two-thirds of Americans* don't have estate planning documents or *even a will*. In fact, *a recent study* found that 30% of Americans don't know if their parents have a will and 40% don't know what's in their parents' will. Yet 60% of Americans told researchers they consider estate planning "important" or "very important."

So why don't more people want to control who manages their assets and takes care of their children? Of course, they love their children, but estate planning can be morbid, confusing and time-consuming. Plus, many people, even those considered affluent, don't feel they're wealthy enough to need an estate plan. A recent *WealthCounsel study* found that three in four American adults (74%) believe estate planning is a "confusing topic." That's just not acceptable.

Among American adults who don't have wills, the top two reasons for their reluctance, *according to Caring.com*, are that they (a) haven't gotten around to it, or (b) don't feel they have enough assets to justify a will or estate plan.

Trust me, those reasons aren't compelling enough to let the courts decide what happens to your assets when you're gone. Don't you want a better outcome for your family when you're no longer there to support them?

For more about estate planning, see my recent post *Can You Keep Ignoring Your Will And Estate Plan?*

FAMILY BANK: A CRITICAL PIECE OF YOUR INTERGENERATIONAL ESTATE PLANNING PUZZLE

As mentioned earlier, a Family Bank is a powerful tool for protecting your family from the consequences of your death or disability, for storing cash that will not lose value, and for helping you finance everything in life including major purchases and investments. However, a Family Bank can also help you support future generations of your family financially so they can reach their goals and dreams. After all, isn't that what we want for our children – to live a fulfilling life and achieve their dreams? Suppose you could guide them on that journey by providing the knowledge, wisdom and resources that help them reach their full potential? Imagine the impact that could have!

In the Family Bank strategy, grandparents can fund life insurance policies for newborn grandchildren. This not only protects them but sustains the Family Bank for the next generation. Once the grandparents pass, their wealth passes to their children, who in turn fund the policies for ***their*** grandchildren...and the cycle continues. Not only will the wealth flow for generations, but it can be shared efficiently in order to make the greatest impact for each individual and for society at large.

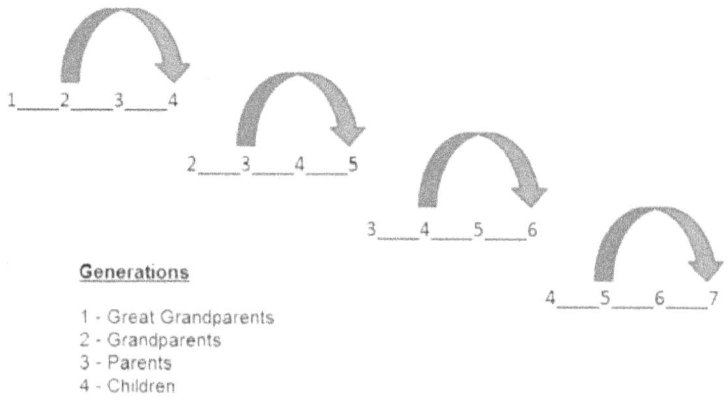

It's very important for parents and grandparents to start teaching the next generation of your family about the Family Bank. It will help them learn about the importance of financing, managing debt, and boosting cash flow while protecting themselves and those they love. Money should not be a taboo subject like it was in my family growing up. There's no specific age for introducing your kids to the Family Bank. But you should certainly be having discussions about basic financial literacy with your kids by middle school or early high school, and then progress from there as circumstances dictate.

TEACHING KIDS ABOUT MONEY

Ron Lieber's book *The Opposite of Spoiled: Raising Kids Who Are Grounded, Generous, and Smart About Money* is a greater tool for parents to use to start teaching their kids about money, family finances, saving, charitable giving and being disciplined about the use of money. It's never too early to start introducing kids to smart money topics such as the basics of saving, spending, and donating money you receive. As your children get older, you can start teaching them about more complex topics such as investing and the role and management of credit and good debt. You can start telling them about some of the things you're doing financially for your own family, so they understand family values and the "why" behind the manner in which you manage your wealth. These lessons will become increasingly important as they mature and start wealth-building journeys for their own families. Unfortunately, many kids – even those from successful, affluent families – never get a proper financial education at an early age, and that lack of wisdom can dog them for the rest of their lives.

By sharing your financial wisdom with the next generation, you will provide them with the tools to create their own future and will ensure they continue the path of prosperity that you started.

KEY LEARNINGS FROM CHAPTER 2:

- Building the right mindset and adopting the right habits is not easy. But if you can do these things, you'll have a tremendous leg up on your pursuit of wealth and a lifetime of meaning.
- Spending time to become more self-aware does not mean you're selfish. It means you're smart and ready to get more out of your relationships with the people you care about most.
- Understanding your "why" can be a great exercise for crystallizing your purpose in life.
- How well do you know your top 5 to 10 values? Without clarity on your values, it's hard to build a life of fulfillment.
- Once you are clear about your values, determine your unique skills, strengths, talents and passions. These are the gifts you should be sharing with the world.
- The most important asset you own is YOU. Are you doing everything you can to protect your No. 1 asset?

- The best investments are not necessarily those with the highest returns. It's about finding the investments that best align with your goals, risk tolerance and stage of life.
- Before investing, ask yourself: (a) "What's the purpose of this investment?" and (b) "What's my level of interest, expertise and experience in this investment?"
- You need not only a portfolio that's diversified, but a mindset than balances short-term thinking with long-term thinking.
- It's essential to familiarize yourself with the power of compounding and the different ***phases*** of the compound interest curve.
- You finance everything you buy in one of two ways: (a) You take on debt and pay back principal (with interest) OR (b) you pay cash and avoid the interest payments.
- Review your estate plan and Family Mission Statement regularly. Don't go another year without having both documents in place – you have too much at stake.
- The Family Bank strategy can provide not only the resources for the next generation but also the financial education to empower them to reach their potential.

Please review the Key Learnings above before moving on to Chapter 3.

CHAPTER THREE

Secure True and Ultimate Freedom

"No one outside ourselves can rule us inwardly. When we know this, we become free."

- Buddha

What does the notion of "ultimate freedom" in life mean to you?

This chapter is about having the power to act, speak, or think without hindrance or restraint.

I was fortunate to have grown up with tremendous freedom in my childhood. As kids, my friends and I were free to roam the streets of my suburban neighborhood without fear or close parental supervision. I don't think the term "helicopter parents" had been invented yet.

Parents weren't nearly as involved in their kids' lives as they are today, and I feel sorry for today's children sometimes. We were given the opportunity to experience life on our terms and to make our own decisions (for better or worse). These days, it would be considered almost criminal to let our children roam the streets on their own. The intense parental involvement in the lives of our children – while well-intentioned – has created unprecedented pressure on our youth. Unfortunately, the helicopter parenting often stunts our children's emotional growth and development.

In our teens and early adulthood, we are strongly encouraged to "grow up" and conform to societal norms: go to a top college, get a good job, buy a big house, raise two and a half children, and put your savings into retirement accounts... and life will be good. But following conventional wisdom can give you less control over your future – and less satisfaction in life.

TIME-STARVED GENERATION

While some people garner great satisfaction from their work – especially in the professional ranks –more and more "successful" people feel time-starved day after day and struggle to balance the various facets of their personal and work lives. Thanks to technology and social media, there are more demands on our time than ever, more distractions than ever and more things competing for our attention than ever.

I know it's hard to believe, but there was a time not long ago when many American families could live relatively comfortably off just one parent's income. Today, both spouses typically must work in order to pay for the most basic needs – not to mention fund the "ideal" lifestyle we see portrayed on social media. Many households borrow heavily from financial institutions to chase that perfect lifestyle (which, unfortunately, can make you feel trapped in your situation without many good options) or even to maintain the most basic level of subsistence. This certainly doesn't sound like the American Dream or the freedom this country was built on. On paper, we're the wealthiest and most prosperous society in our nation's history, but we've evolved into a society that "doesn't have time" for the things we want in life.

What this boils down to is using our two most precious resources – time and capital – as effectively as we can to serve our personal needs and to create freedom in our lives.

KEY STEP 9: BE RESPONSIBLE FOR YOUR OWN FREEDOM

One book that really exemplifies the concept of freedom is Viktor Frankl's *Man's Search for Meaning*. After having every human dignity stripped away from him in German concentration camps and having everything that he loved destroyed, Frankl asked himself: "How does a human still feel free?

Frankl's book resonated with me because having the freedom to be myself and to make my own choices about my life's direction is critically important to me. Finding meaning in that choice is what ultimately sets us free. We are responsible for our choices. As a result, we are all responsible for our own freedom, even if it is an internal freedom.

It's easy to make excuses and blame others for a less-than-satisfying life, but ultimately you are responsible for your own happiness and sense of freedom. Without taking full control of the direction of your life, you will always be vulnerable to external forces that can derail your plans and dreams. If your car is rolling down the highway at a high rate of speed, would you rather be in the driver's seat or the passenger seat? I'm sure most of you would say the driver's seat. So, take the wheel and drive toward your destiny.

FINANCIAL FOOTPRINTS

If you think about it, there's a tug-of-war over your money every single day. You have your own plans for your money, but corporate advertisers, financial institutions, and the IRS are trying to control and use your money, too – and maybe even a jealous ex-spouse or unscrupulous creditors. Yes, it will take some effort and energy to discover where this is happening in your life, but once you do, you can explore alternative approaches to break free or at least minimize their control.

NOTE: My book ***Hidden Wealth Eroders*** talks about this extensively and describes what you can do about it.

One of the most important things to understand is that financial institutions are playing by a different set of rules than you are. They want your money, they want it often, they hold it for long periods of time, and they only give it back to you on their terms, which means very slowly. Most people wouldn't put up with a relationship that's all take and no give, but we've been conditioned to think we don't have any alternatives when it comes to the financial institutions we use.

Perhaps that's why so many Americans head into retirement without having saved nearly enough for their post-working years, even if they dramatically reduce their living expenses. Even if they have saved money diligently throughout their working lives, it doesn't give them much financial freedom if they can't access that money without facing severe penalties. I know what you're thinking. Isn't the ability to delay gratification a desired trait? Not necessarily. This "deferral" mentality has seeped into our society as the optimal approach to managing one's wealth. In other words, sacrifice now for enjoyment later.

But it doesn't have to be a zero-sum game. Suppose you could have enjoyment and access to your money now as well as in retirement?

It all starts with building a strong foundation for your financial life, which requires full protection of your assets through insurance (P&C, Disability, Life, Umbrella), estate planning and savings (liquidity). This goes back to implementing the Hierarchy of Wealth model we discussed in Chapter 1 to ensure your financial foundation is rock solid. A rock-solid financial foundation gives you the ability to withstand anything that comes your way and continue to succeed financially. Having a plan is great – but expect that your plan will not go exactly as planned, and you'll have safeguards to ensure you prosper no matter what the situation is.

A key part of the financial foundation is committing 10% to 15% of your income for retirement and always having a "rainy day" emergency fund of at least six months' worth of living expenses. But that's not all. We strongly advise our clients to have a third bucket of money available at all times for great opportunities that come their way. We like to call this your "opportunity fund."

Life is unpredictable. But those who have taken steps to solidify their financial foundation will also have the peace of mind to handle financial setbacks and reversals, and the freedom to take advantage of great investment opportunities that came their way unexpectedly – opportunities that most people cannot seize unless they are willing to put their financial plan in jeopardy.

Again, that's why it's so important to focus your investments on things you thoroughly understand and can control, such as your business as well as real estate and your personal development. ***Please refer to Tier 2 of their Hierarchy of Wealth pyramid in Chapter 1.***

"Luck is what happens when preparation meets opportunity."
– Roman Philosopher Seneca

KEY STEP 10: USE YOUR TIME AND RESOURCES WISELY

How often do you find yourself thinking, "I don't have enough time to do the things I want in life"? So many pressures both personally and professionally are vying for your time and are potentially taking you away from the important things in life.

How often do you feel like you're on that hamster wheel during the workweek and simply living for the weekend just so you can take a deep breath? If so, you're certainly not alone, but is this any way to live your life?

How many hours during a week are potentially being wasted on things that don't serve your purpose, your values, or your priorities? If you kept a time journal of a typical week in your life, you might be surprised to see how many.

I've been a student of time (and time management) for many years. I still have a long way to go when it comes to managing my precious time more effectively, but I've learned some valuable lessons along the way. Here is a summary:

1. We all have the same 24 hours in a day – the same 168 hours per week – but we never know when our clock will stop.
2. Plan your weeks and days in advance so they align to your key priorities and the goals you're trying to reach (both personal and professional).
3. Minimize social media, gaming, sports gambling and other mobile phone distractions.
4. Say NO to more things than you say YES to. Guard your time incessantly – it's one of the most valuable assets you have.

One of the best ways to break out of the time-famine trap of that hamster wheel is to spend a little time every day focusing on your short-term and long-term goals. Each day, each week and each month in your life counts. Don't waste any of them.

REMEMBER SUNDAY PLANNING

As discussed in Chapter 1, one exercise I've found very helpful for keeping my sanity involves dedicating time every Sunday afternoon to mapping out my priorities and goals for the week ahead. Yes, even a hardcore football fans like me, can find some time for Sunday Planning and still spend quality time with my family, golfing buddies, NFL fans and fellow worshippers at my church.

I realize it's easy to feel overwhelmed when you're staring at a blank sheet of paper designed for planning. So, I focus on just my ***three main goals*** for the year and identify the things I must absolutely get done in the week ahead to move that yearly goal forward. This exercise forces me to prioritize on what's absolutely most important and not get sidetracked by all the sideshows, rabbit holes and digital temptations that stand in my way.

In addition to my Sunday planning session, I spend a few minutes at the start of each day to put two or three high-priority items on my calendar. I try to devote 60-90 minutes, two or three times per day, to each of those top priorities. I've found this process very helpful for focusing my attention on where it needs to be. Even better, it requires me to say NO to things that are NOT one of my top priorities. I think you'll also find it helpful or navigating that very difficult gray area of things that are "important" but not absolutely urgent. ***Learning to say no to the wrong things is just important to as saying yes to the right things.***

Entire books and seminars have been devoted to time management. Simon Wright's book *The Power of Saying No* is one I've found helpful.

Finally, you have to give your brain frequent rests in order to remain optimally focused. Well-known business coach Dan Sullivan, who was introduced in Chapter 1, preaches the importance of having (a) Focus Days, (b) Buffer Days and (c) Free Days during the week, to avoid burnout and to give your brain time to revitalize.

(a) On **Focus Days**, you must commit to hitting the most important things on your priority list in order to move your live and business forward.
(b) **Buffer Days** are used to help you prepare for your Focus Days.
(c) **Free Days** can be spent doing whatever you please, as long as it relaxes you and allows you to recharge.

I've learned the hard way that running full steam without a break for extended periods of time puts you on the fast track to burnout. Having intentional breaks throughout the day (and week) will give you the energy to remain focused on your priorities and help you attain a more balanced life.

FINANCIAL FOOTPRINTS

When it comes to our financial lives, who wouldn't want to have more wealth so they can possess and pursue things in life they desire? While most people talk about possessions and passions, what they're really talking about is having more time – more time to enjoy life, their families, hobbies and experiences. However, as we noted earlier, most people are experiencing headwinds with their money, which makes it hard to achieve financial success and freedom. Fortunately, there are some fundamental ways to get you on a better path with tailwinds in your favor.

1. IDENTIFY THE FINANCIAL LEAKS THAT ARE HINDERING YOUR ABILITY TO BUILD WEALTH

We've introduced the concept of financial leaks in my aforementioned book ***Hidden Wealth Eroders***. One of the most damaging leaks we all face is Opportunity Cost – the loss of positive benefit A when you decide to go with option B instead.

Here are three examples of Opportunity Cost from my book about wealth eroders:

(a) Paying more than your fair share in taxes. Each dollar you pay in tax is essentially a loss. That's because that money paid to Uncle Sam is no longer available to create wealth for you. There are numerous ways to reduce your tax bill (legally) by following the laws put forth by the IRS and the incentives they want to encourage. Here are some examples:

1. Start a business and create jobs.
2. Own rental real estate to provide a place for people to live.
3. Donate to charities.
4. Protect your family from premature death.
5. Invest in the discovery of natural resources (e.g., oil and gas).

(b) Having way too much cash stuck in a low-interest checking or savings account. Any extra cash you may have could be put to much better use paying down debt or building your retirement nest egg. With inflation eroding our wealth every day, storing your money in low-interest "safe" accounts is actually not that safe when you're guaranteed to lose money. The best place we've found to store "safe" dollars and to keep them accessible is a high-cash-value whole life insurance policy. These policies are a foundational piece of the Family Bank strategy and allow you to recapture interest that would otherwise have gone to banks.

(c) Outliving your term insurance. If you're just paying for term insurance, that expires after 20 years and is never used 98% of the time. Then you have to pay significantly more later in life to continue to be covered. Instead, you could be investing in a policy that builds wealth and borrowing capacity – while also providing a death benefit.

2. HAVE YOUR DOLLARS DOING AS MANY JOBS AS POSSIBLE

Typical financial advice instructs us to put our money into accounts that are only used for one job – saving exclusively for college or saving exclusively for retirement. On the surface that makes sense, but what if you need that money for something else? Suppose you could have your money doing a host of jobs at the same time to protect and build your wealth? The Family Bank strategy is a great example. In a Family Bank, the same dollar contributed to your account can be used to protect against death, disability, taxes and creditors, while also providing a productive place to store money for growth potential – AND providing a guaranteed source of easy financing that allows you to invest your money to build even greater wealth …or transfer it to others tax-advantageously. That's why I call the Family Bank a "financial Swiss army knife"!

3. ENSURE YOUR DOLLARS CONTINUE TO FLOW - INSTEAD OF ACCUMULATING

The flow of money can be like a river, cascading toward a larger body of water. Put another way, cash flow breathes life into your financial plan. In his aforementioned book Rich Dad Poor Dad, Robert Kiyosaki argues that wealthy people think about money very differently than middle-class people do and they manage it very differently as well. You can see how their cash-flow patterns differ in their Income Statements and Balance Sheets (see examples below):

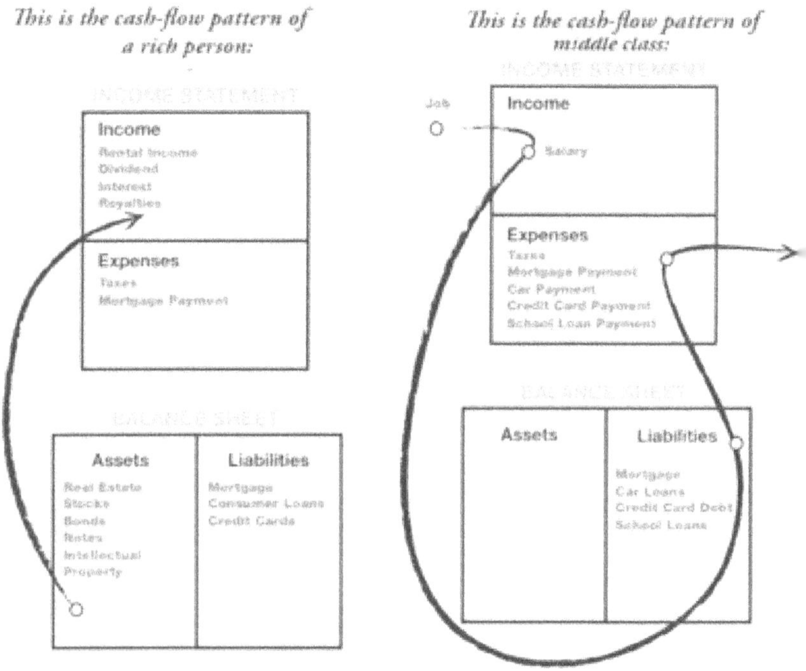

Source: Rich Dad Poor Dad: What the Rich Teach Their Kids About Money That the Poor and Middle Class Do Not!

According to Kiyosaki, many middle-class Americans use debt to help fund their lifestyles. They use debt to secure things they need and want, and a large portion of their employment income is used to pay for those things. They generate very little income outside of their paychecks. More troubling, they pay the highest relative taxes and owe the most in expenses and interest to financial institutions. Additionally, the "assets" that middle-class people tend to own (e.g., house, 401(k), IRA) don't generate any usable income for them today. They can only accumulate those assets for future use, and those assets are potentially subject to even higher taxes later in life.

By contrast, the wealthy understand the power of building assets that can generate usable income today AND in the future. When income comes into their lives, they utilize it to secure assets that can generate additional income (e.g., businesses, real estate) and often tax benefits. Additionally, wealthy people know how to leverage "good debt" to help them fuel investments in areas for which they have expertise or good partnerships.

GOOD DEBT vs. BAD DEBT

"Good debt" is not an oxymoron. Good debt is used to purchase assets that can create income and wealth. For instance, purchasing a rental property with low-interest fixed debt can generate cash flow, provide tax advantages, and help you pay down debt and build wealth. You're not really in debt if your asset value is greater than the loan balance you've taken on – you simply HAVE debt.

By contrast, bad debt is any type of interest-bearing loan you use to finance your lifestyle. For example, when you're not paying off your credit card in full every month, you're paying extremely high interest to the card issuer and not paying down the principal. This simply enriches the card issuer (usually a bank) and makes it very difficult for you to save adequately for your future.

Middle-class people focus on accumulating assets for later use and keep much of their wealth in the hands of financial institutions. By contrast, the wealthy focus on ensuring cash flow from their assets (e.g., businesses, real estate, private loans) and are constantly working to generate greater returns. They have learned to leverage other people's money (e.g., that of financial institutions and the IRS) to build wealth and achieve greater control over their lives.

KEY STEP 11: CREATE OPTIONS AND NOT JUST CHOICES / CONSEQUENCES

Prepare for the worst, so you'll be able to withstand any storms that come your way. As the old saying goes: "An ounce of prevention is worth a pound of cure."

In the business world, project managers call this a "**pre-mortem.**" This is when you try to anticipate anything that could possibly fail, and then plan in advance to defend against those threats. The pre-mortem strategy can be applied to just about anything of importance in your life, including buying a home, starting a business and certainly making financial decisions. I know it's unsettling at times, but anticipating worst-case scenarios (e.g., long-term disability, death, lawsuits, job loss) and how you would handle them – before they happen – will give you concrete steps to address them and will help you sleep better at night.

Visit Riskology for more about the pre-mortem technique.
If you've made it this far in this book, I sincerely appreciate the commitment of time and mental energy you've given me. At this point, you're ready to explore ways to strengthen your mindset too, so you can think calmly and rationally during any crisis and not let runaway emotions control you.

I'm a strong advocate of thinking positively and focusing on the good things in life, but I'm also a realist. There is only so much we can control in our lives, and things can change in a heartbeat. No one plans to have an accident or experience a natural disaster, for instance, but those things happen all the time without warning. Some people never recover from these major setbacks in life, but as mentioned earlier, such setbacks don't have to ruin us if we prepare for them rationally. Further, life's major setbacks can even allow us to take advantage of an opportunity that never would have occurred to us. Plan for your plan to not always go according to plan.

REAL-WORLD EXAMPLE

For example, what if your company is undergoing a reorganization and your position has been eliminated? For many, this can be a scary time and cause some serious worry and anxiety. However, what if you assumed this was a possibility and you prepared for it? In that case, you have ample savings to access, you've been updating your resume along the way, and you've started to consider alternative jobs or business opportunities that you're interested in or passionate about – or you've developed other forms of income streams to supplement your lifestyle. This could open up opportunities to design the lifestyle and working situation that would truly be fulfilling for you. With the right motivation and support, your opportunities for success would be limitless.

There's a philosophy called stoicism (mentioned in Chapter 1) that teaches you to be rational in times of crisis and actually learn to turn life's setbacks into opportunities. Humans are emotional beings. It's not a sign of weakness to have an emotional reaction to a situation. What Stoics want you to understand is that you cannot allow runaway emotions to make decisions for you, as that often leads to mistakes and panic.

Again, Holiday's book *The Obstacle Is the Way* teaches us to regain control of our emotions during stressful situations so that we can think – and make decisions – rationally. One idea is to take a situation and pretend it's not happening to you. When we remove ourselves from the equation, we can be more objective when assessing a situation and evaluating options.

Let's say a close friend is very worried about losing their job. The stress of that situation can elicit emotions ranging from fear and worry to anger and frustration, all of which are understandable. However, as someone viewing it from the outside, you can see that the friend can take necessary steps to prepare, such as getting their resume together or touching base with their network to explore opportunities. By being proactive and rational, rather than consumed by fear, your friend is positioning themselves well to handle a difficult life transition and potentially find a much better career opportunity.

This type of resilience also comes from having a growth mindset to recognize that you can continue to learn anything if you put your mind to it. This process might take you down the road of starting your own business or consulting in areas in which you have unique expertise. As the saying goes, "There is strength in numbers." Expanding your network continuously can give you the strength and support you need to get through the most difficult times in your personal and professional life.

THE POWER OF A STRONG NETWORK

Whether you are faced with death, divorce, a health setback, or a financial setback, having a strong network of family, friends, and professional colleagues in place will substantially boost your spirits and help you stay grounded during tough times. You don't want to go through these difficult times alone.

Ultimately, we need to take responsibility for the direction of our own lives, but it's very important to have other people in your life with whom you can collaborate, so you can support each other's dreams and goals. With that support in place, you can follow the Stoics' philosophy of turning a potentially bad situation into a great opportunity.

FINANCIAL FOOTPRINTS

In order to give yourself and your family more options, you want to maximize the protection of your assets, health and family so you can overcome any obstacle that comes your way and ensure that the people closest to you can live their best lives. But most financial advice is focused simply on what you need to get by in terms of protections or retirement income -- rather than on what you truly want.

What I don't like about this mindset is that it's based on scarcity rather than abundance. It's a zero-sum game in which someone else has to lose in order for you to win. If you always feel there is never enough wealth to go around, you will avoid risk at all costs and never explore opportunities that can be more lucrative.

Focusing on what you truly want gives you the power to think more creatively and expansively about your options. It puts you in a position to achieve a life of abundance. When you feel you have an abundant life, you will be more open to new experiences and ideas that you would never have considered or encountered with a scarcity mindset.

Yes, getting what you truly want in life may come at a cost, but that's why it's so important to explore ways to manage your wealth more efficiently. Doing so will ensure that your money is working as hard as you are to build your family wealth rather than enriching others.

TWO CRITICAL PATHS IN YOUR FINANCIAL LIFE: PROTECTION AND WEALTH ACCUMULATION

Without being fully protected, you leave yourself and your assets highly vulnerable to things you cannot control. Why not spend a little money protecting your wealth so you and your family are more resilient to death, disability, lawsuits, divorce and other major setbacks in life? Most people are so focused on building wealth that they forget how to protect it. Life is full of the unexpected. Unfortunately, you only need to get blindsided once to have your lifelong wealth-building efforts severely compromised. Remember, even the best laid plans rarely go according to plan. By preparing for the worst-case scenario and taking the steps to protect yourself and your family, you will significantly increase your odds of achieving financial success.

As mentioned earlier, you always want to have at least six months of living expenses on hand in a highly liquid "rainy day" account that you only use for emergencies. Some of our clients keep 12 months of living expenses in their rainy-day accounts, and others keep several years' worth. Everyone has a different situation and needs. But having instant liquidity at all times will give you the peace of mind to get through the tough times.

Ready cash, however, is not all about doom and gloom. I'm also a firm believer in having an opportunity fund of readily available cash in a separate account. Just as life throws unexpected setbacks your way, it also sends you unexpected business and investment opportunities. You want separate, ready cash accounts on hand for both situations, so you can always protect yourself while never missing out on great opportunities to build your wealth.

Unfortunately, even many affluent, successful people have all of their money tied up in their house, retirement accounts and long-term investments, so they don't have much liquidity. Without that liquidity, you don't have much flexibility in your life. The best place we've found to store emergency cash AND opportunity cash is a Family Bank.

WHAT YOU CAN LEARN FROM THE HABITS OF MILLIONAIRES

For his book *Rich Habits*, Tom Corley did an extensive five-year study of the rich and poor. He found that while the ultra-rich gained their wealth in a wide variety of ways, self-made millionaires tended to have similar traits when it comes to their relationship with money:

- **65% of self-made millionaires had three streams of income**
- **45% of self-made millionaires had four streams of income**
- **29% of self-made millionaires had five or more streams of income**

In other words, they don't rely on a single stream of income (such as a job) or just two streams (job and retirement account).

When most Americans join the full-time workforce, they are taught to put a portion of their income into retirement accounts that they cannot access for decades (e.g., 401(k)s, IRAs) and to wait patiently as it (hopefully) accumulates through compounding. In a society like ours that encourages conspicuous consumption, company-sponsored retirement accounts are a great way to force workers to save a portion of their income for retirement that might otherwise be lost through spending. However, the truly wealthy know that keeping your money moving at all times and creating "velocity" is the key to building wealth.

Building or securing assets that bring you income in different ways will give you more flexibility to change course and secure a life you truly desire. Imagine if your hard-working dollars start bringing back their "friends" to help your wealth-building cause in the form of different streams of income while you sleep?

That's not a pipe dream; that's essentially what the wealthy do.

KEY LEARNINGS FROM CHAPTER 3:

- One of the keys to having a life of abundance is using your two most precious resources – time and capital – as effectively as possible.
- It's easy to make excuses and blame others for a less-than-satisfying life, but ultimately you are responsible for your own happiness and sense of freedom.
- Without taking full control of the direction of your life, you will always be vulnerable to external forces that can derail your plans and dreams.
- Financial institutions play by a different set of rules than you do in relationships. They want your money, they want it often, they hold it for long periods of time and they only give it back to you on their terms, i.e., very slowly. Why put up with such a one-sided relationship?
- You not only need six months' worth of living expenses in a fund for emergencies, but you need an equal amount in a dedicated "opportunity fund" to take advantage of great opportunities that come your way unexpectedly.
- Don't succumb to time famine. Sunday Planning is a simple exercise for mapping out your priorities and goals for the week ahead.
- Identify the financial leaks that are hindering your ability to build wealth, and make sure your money is always working as hard as you are.

- There are two critical paths in your financial life: protection and wealth accumulation.
- Understand the difference between good debt and bad debt.
- We all face difficult setbacks in life. Responding the right way to those setbacks can greatly boost your spirits and keep you on the path to success.
- By creating multiple streams of income, you'll have more flexibility to finance everything in life, even when the unexpected hits your world.

Please review the Key Learnings above before moving on to Chapter 4.

CHAPTER FOUR

See The Good

"Acknowledging the good that you already have in your life is the foundation for all abundance."
- Eckhart Tolle

Life is incredibly hectic these days. It can be difficult to find the time to reflect on your good fortune and to appreciate all the progress you have made toward a comfortable and rewarding future. It can be especially tough for successful, motivated people like you to stop and smell the roses when you're conditioned to always seek more…more money, more prestige, more stuff.

My parents' experiences, described in the Introduction of this book, pushed me to take ownership not only of my financial life but of my non-financial life as well. It's been an ongoing learning experience for me and will continue to be so for my remaining days on earth.

If nothing else, I've learned to focus on the good things in life and to feel gratitude for my good fortune. Trust me, gratitude is not something that came naturally to me, as I was always extremely hard on myself. Fear of failure was always top of mind for me, and I tended to dwell on my mistakes and shortcomings rather than appreciate all the "wins" and good fortune I had.

Only through my own exploration and experience have I come to realize how limiting that type of thinking was to my happiness and success in life. These are lessons I try to pass on to my two teenage sons.

There are many experts who believe, like me, that having a positive mindset can lead to greater outcomes, because it can be a motivating force to help you handle the challenges that come your way. I'm not saying that thinking positive thoughts alone will bring those things to you, as this still requires your effort and actions to make it happen, but I do believe that a positive attitude provides strong support as you push forward.

Dan Sullivan has written often the gap between what you have achieved so far in life and what you have not achieved. People tend to obsess about what they haven't achieved (or acquired) so much that they can't let themselves enjoy what they have achieved (or acquired).

Focusing on what you haven't achieved yet can lead to frustration and disappointment. Yes, it's good to reach for goals and think into the future and what you want to achieve, but it's key to not forget and appreciate how far you've come already, and to recognize you're on a journey instead of just trying to reach a destination.

Unfortunately, we are bombarded 24/7 with information, news, and opinions from so-called experts. While the internet has given us instant access to an incredible wealth of information, it also can be a burden. So much of the news, data, and opinions we get are tilted toward the negative. Internet companies and the news media know that fear and crisis draw more clicks and ratings than feel-good news, but constant exposure to negativity can wear down even the most optimistic among us.

Research shows we tend to...

1. Pay more attention to *negative events* than to positive ones.
2. Learn more from *negative outcomes and experiences*.

3. *Make decisions* based on negative information more than on positive data.

If these negative biases above sound familiar to you, don't despair. It's part of your DNA to protect yourself from perceived threats. This goes back to prehistoric times. It just means we have to be proactive about focusing on the positive things in life to avoid living in a constant state of fear and pessimism. I realize this mindset comes more easily to some people than it does to others. As the saying goes, "Perception is reality." When we feel like we're constantly under a dark cloud, our willingness to act decisively and work through true crises and setbacks is impacted.

Making a conscious effort to focus on the positive aspects of life can help you overcome challenges and better position yourself to withstand storms. More important, an optimistic mindset will drive you to higher levels of greatness with more confidence and passion. Sometimes it's a good idea to stop and smell the roses.

KEY STEP 12: PRACTICE GRATITUDE FREQUENTLY TO BREED HAPPINESS

Remember Shawn Achor (*The Happiness Advantage*) from Chapter 2? The best-selling author believes that many people assume happiness comes only after they have achieved professional success and gained substantial wealth. That's not actually true, as Achor shows, and I couldn't agree more. I can tell you from personal experience that happiness is something you can control and build for yourself at any stage of life, regardless of your career and financial situation. As Achor argues, fostering a positive mindset will lead you down a path of finding what you're truly passionate about and how you're uniquely able to contribute positively to society. This increases the chance that you will stay engaged, continue to grow and learn, and find fulfillment, Achor adds.

When I achieved a level of wealth I originally thought equated to success and therefore happiness, I honestly didn't feel that much different. Yes, I felt a sense of accomplishment from reaching that goal and being able to provide for my family, but I didn't feel any joy. While my bank account was robust, I didn't have any sense of purpose in my life, so the extra money was meaningless. My journey to a sense of purpose took many years, but eventually I came to the realization that by maintaining a positive outlook, by doing things that brought me energy and by helping others with their financial concerns, I could find happiness and fulfillment. The money simply followed.

In my experience, this is also a great reminder of the importance of having an abundant mindset instead of a scarcity mindset, as I discussed starting all the way back in the Introduction of this book.

Again, the notion of "abundance" was developed by our friend Stephen Covey (*The Seven Habits of Highly Effective People*), as discussed in Chapter 2. According to Covey, abundance is a mindset in which a person believes there are "enough resources and successes to share with others." Compare that to what Covey calls the *scarcity* mindset, which is based on the idea that life is a zero-sum game – if someone else wins or is successful in a situation, then someone else has to lose.

By staying focused on abundance rather than scarcity, you can explore opportunities in life with confidence and continue to progress and learn.

It's important to practice gratitude and to have an abundance mindset as often as you can. In our society, wealth is often equated with success and prestige. Let me tell you from firsthand experience that becoming wealthier will not necessarily make you happier. That's especially true if the pursuit of wealth comes at the expense of the other important things in your life.

FINANCIAL FOOTPRINTS

My definition of wealth is about more than money; it's about having an abundance of everything you want in life. It could be anything from being healthy and having strong relationships with family and friends to having sufficient time for your hobbies, passions and community. Of course, having enough money to live the life you truly desire is part of that equation.

It starts with taking an honest look at your finances. Start by evaluating all the financial pieces of your life, including your **Protections** (assets, health, life), your **Savings** (money that is safe and accessible), your **Growth** (investments), your **Debt** and your **Cash Flow**. Most people don't look at these important areas holistically to ensure they are working together in the most efficient manner.

As you evaluate where you stand with respect to these important aspects of your financial life, ask yourself in which of these areas you feel good. What are you most proud of? Even if an area seems minor (e.g., having three months' worth of living expenses in a ready-cash emergency fund), use that win as a happiness benchmark from which you can plan future improvements and progress. Without showing gratitude for all the good things you have already attained, it's difficult to build momentum for the goals you want to pursue down the road.

KEY STEP 13: CLOSE THE GAP BETWEEN WHERE YOU ARE NOW AND WHERE YOU WANT TO BE

Unfortunately, in our fast-paced competitive society, many people focus only on what they think is lacking in their lives and forget to appreciate how far they have come. Social media has only exacerbated this situation. Do you really think everyone's life is as perfect as they'd have you believe on their curated, filtered social media accounts? Of course not.

Still, this distorted view of social capital and influence makes most people feel inadequate. This negative mindset prevents you from being thankful for the many gifts you've received in life, and it will keep pushing you in the wrong direction. The feeling of "never enough" is what Covey's scarcity mindset is all about.

That's why it's so important to take time to smell the roses and appreciate what you've accomplished on a daily, weekly, and yearly basis. Take a moment to reflect on the past few months or the past year. This can be a formal review – done individually or with your family – to identify the progress you have made toward your goals and where things may have fallen short. The more honest you can be with yourself (and family), the more you'll get out of this exercise. This will help you close some of the gaps that have been keeping you from attaining your life goals.

"Success is the progressive realization of a worthy ideal."
– Earl Nightingale, Author and Radio Host

FINANCIAL FOOTPRINTS

Doing periodic reviews of your financial statements, insurance policies, savings accounts, net worth and even financial literacy is a wise move from a protection standpoint. Whether you do this with the help of an advisor is up to you. The key is to do your reviews on a consistent quarterly or yearly basis, and to assess the progress you've made toward your wealth-building and retirement goals. This exercise will also open your eyes to new opportunities in your financial life. Make sure to celebrate the progress you've made in the areas of highest importance to you and your family.

For example, perhaps you've made great progress in paying down credit card debt, with a goal of paying off all of your high-interest cards in full by the end of the year. That's great, but you could also use the review to evaluate new opportunities, such as learning how to use "good debt" to build your wealth even further. For more about this, review **Good debt vs. bad debt** in Chapter 3 (in Key Step 10).

It's easy to dwell on what you haven't achieved at the expense of what you ***have*** achieved. Don't fall into that trap. Celebrating your progress, not lamenting your shortcomings, will do more to push you forward. Make sure to celebrate even the small wins such as saving extra money or paying down some debt. Building wealth is not an overnight game for most people, so recognizing even minor progress can be a great motivator to keep pushing forward.

When it comes to your finances, I suggest taking an assessment of where you are from an income and net worth perspective. Try to do your assessment quarterly, if not annually. Doing so will uncover areas that need to be addressed but will also show the progress you're making toward your goals. Your quarterly (or annual) review may not be monumental each time you do it, but it will help you spot wins – and areas where you can course-correct.

KEY STEP 14: CONTROL YOUR ATTITUDE AND EFFORT

There are so many things we cannot control, but I've found there are two things you CAN control:

1. **Your attitude**
2. **Your effort**

It's important to have the goals and outcomes you want to have in your life (e.g., perfect weight, net worth), but these are a result of having the right attitude, beliefs, and actions on a consistent and constant basis. That's why I firmly believe that to achieve anything you want, you must have the right attitude in place, which will drive the actions and results you seek. Thankfully, with focus and practice, you can develop your attitude into one that lifts you up instead of keeping you down.

YOUR ATTITUDE

A positive attitude is an essential habit to develop. Regardless of what you're doing (whether it's enjoyable or unpleasant), having a positive attitude will allow you to take something positive from any life experience – including unpleasant ones. For instance, taking an entry-level job may not seem glamorous, but it can teach you about a company's work environment and business strategy. It can also allow you to meet new people who can mentor you. Entry-level jobs may also help you learn about tasks and job roles that you definitely DON'T want to do in the future. Don't underestimate the value of that!

When you feel yourself drifting toward negativity, look for ways to break the cycle by asking yourself the following questions:

1. What's the best I can hope for given what I know right now?
2. How can I use my strengths and skills to meet this challenge?
3. What can I ***NOT*** do at this time?
4. What kind of person/leader do I want/not want to be?

YOUR EFFORT

You can't control outcomes, but you can control how you show up each day and the work you do. For instance, common advice is to drink at least eight glasses of water each day. Water is inexpensive and readily available in our country, but most people still don't drink enough water. It's easier for most people to select another beverage that has more taste. Even if they go for water, they don't have a disciplined way of keeping track of how many glasses they've consumed.

This is where daily disciplines come into play. Whether it's eating right, exercising, reading or spending more quality time with your family, daily habits that support your goals and vision in life require persistence and intentional focus. Relying on willpower alone will be difficult, so creating habits that you don't have to think about is key.

Anything worth doing will often come with challenges

When I ask people what superpower they would most like to have, they often say, "Being able to clone myself" or "Being able to read people's minds." But I rarely hear people say, "Being more resilient in the face of adversity" or "Not being afraid to lean into challenges." Based on the success of books such as Nassim Taleb's *Antifragile* or Dr. Paige Williams' *Becoming AntiFragile: Learning to Thrive through Disruption, Challenge and Change*, which was introduced in Chapter 1, you'd think gaining "antifragile" superpowers would be top of mind for many people. But it isn't. Maybe it should be.

What I love about antifragility is that it takes the focus away from external factors (that we cannot control). Doing so puts the emphasis on things we CAN control, such as having the right attitudes, mindsets and energy so we can become stronger by turning adversity into opportunities.

If it were easy to set big goals or make major changes in our life, we'd all do it. But life is always filled with obstacles and setbacks. We cannot predict when and how they will occur, but if you acknowledge that potholes and speedbumps are inevitable in the highway of life, then you can learn to persevere when others choose to give up. Success in life comes with being able to lean into difficult situations rather than run away from them, so you come out stronger at the end.

Suppose you lose your job. Yes, it can be an awful situation and may be financially and emotionally painful in the short run. But if losing your job is the catalyst that makes you finally pursue something you always wanted to do (e.g., start a business), then that's an opportunity more than a setback – don't you agree? Same setback, different outcome. It all depends on your point of view and how well you've prepared. Making the most out of a bad situation can make you stronger for the next obstacles that come your way...and you know there will always be new ones coming.

FINANCIAL FOOTPRINTS

Remember, it's all about attitude and effort. Many people believe personal finance is complicated, and it can be...if you let it overwhelm you. But by maintaining a positive attitude, putting in the effort, and developing a growth-minded approach and a long-term view, you can build your financial acumen slowly but steadily over time. Start with the basics:

- Spend less than you make.
- Consistently save a portion of your wealth.

- Maintain access to ready cash for emergencies and opportunities.
- Only invest in things you understand (and can control).

The key is to build these into habits that you can continue for the long haul.

When it comes to good money habits, most people know they have to save for retirement and for their children's higher education. But when people look at "their number" for retirement or college tuition, the goal can seem out of reach. However, if you know you have to contribute X% of your paycheck to retirement and college saving on the 15th and 30th of the month, it becomes an automatic (good) habit. It's something you do without having to think about it. That's how you gain a sense of control when your willpower is failing, and when you're tempted to spend that money on a shopping splurge or a new "toy."

When you treat your personal financial life as a business – with you as the CEO and your financial advisor as the CFO – it's far easier to pinpoint areas that need to be improved. Becoming antifragile will help.

One of the core principles of antifragility is that in today's highly unpredictable world, you can't protect yourself from every bad thing that happens. Instead of feeling sorry for yourself, focus on controlling what you can control and letting go of things you can't control. More important, when disruption does occur in your life, don't run away from it. Instead, lean into it so you not only survive but learn, thrive and gain from that disruption.

That's why it's key to build a strong financial foundation (*review Tier 1 of the Hierarchy of Wealth pyramid*) that starts with protecting your assets, income and life, and also to have separate emergency funds and opportunity funds. This also includes addressing any "bad debt" you may have taken on to support your lifestyle (e.g., your high-interest credit cards).

This is where the Family Bank strategy is critical. Not only will it protect you and your family in the event of death or disability, but it provides a great place to store wealth without loss. A Family Bank also provides a guaranteed financing arm that you can utilize for purchases and investments. Even better, you can access the money (and pay it back) on your terms, not on a big financial institution's terms.

Having the protection side of your financial life in place will put you in a better position to invest opportunistically in Tier 2 so you have more ownership and control – and less risk. This includes investing in your personal development, in a business or even in real estate. Again, by investing in things you understand and can control, you will reduce your risk and greatly increase your chance of success.

When it comes to your finances, you need the same drive to keep getting better. That involves practicing good money habits each and every day. You need the discipline to save consistently and to make smart financing decisions for ***everything*** you buy – or hope to purchase. **Good habits are like smart investing. Small, consistent steps in the right direction will compound over time to your benefit.**

KEY STEP 15: COMPETE WITH YOURSELF, NOT WITH OTHERS

We all want to know how we stack up to our peers. The idea of keeping up with the Joneses has been around forever, but it has created unprecedented levels of anxiety today thanks to social media and the perfectly curated lives those in our circle can manufacture online. We know what we see on people's social platforms is far from reality, but we can't seem to look away. This only makes us feel inadequate and/or jealous.

As motivational speaker Jim Rohn liked to say: ***"Don't wish it was easier; wish you were better."***

What he meant was this: you should strive to be better each and every day, and to be very clear about who you want to become and why. You were put on this earth for a simple reason: to become the best version of yourself for your family and others in your inner circle, at the highest level possible.

Thanks to social media, everyone seems to be incredibly wealthy, beautiful, healthy and living a perfect life. When comparing ourselves to our peers online, it's natural to feel deficient. Same goes for our finances.

FINANCIAL FOOTPRINTS

I've learned the hard way that having wealth without purpose is just another form of poverty. In the pursuit of wealth and success, make sure you're building a life of meaning. It's not just about accumulating more money and more stuff.

Wealth isn't what will bring you happiness; wealth is a tool that will help you attain the life you truly desire. As Shawn Achor has said, "Happiness is what will drive you to success." And as the Greek philosopher Epictetus said, "Wealth consists not in having great possessions, but in having few wants."

By maintaining a positive outlook, I've found, you will feel more fulfilled and can more easily reach your true potential in all aspects of your life than if you spend time dwelling on what's missing from your life. While many people are considered wealthy based on their bank accounts, they would not be considered wealthy based on their lives, relationships and health. True wealth is an abundance of what you want to achieve in any area of your life.

"When wealth is lost, nothing is lost; when health is lost, something is lost; when character is lost, all is lost."
– Billy Graham

Although you may not be exactly where you want to be financially, think about things you can be proud of. Think about some of the world's most successful people: Oprah, Michael Jordan, Tom Brady, Elon Musk, to name a few. They're at the absolute top of their respective fields, but what they have in common is that they never stop trying to get better each and every day. In some ways, their toughest competitors are themselves, the voices in their heads.

If you take away nothing else from this guide, remember this: don't succumb to keeping up with the Joneses. Their financial needs and wants are likely very different from your family's. The most important thing is to stick to your plan when the rest of the world is trying to distract you – to be crystal clear about what you value and what brings you fulfillment.

As noted throughout this guide, to start taking steps in the right direction, you'll want to be very honest with yourself about where you are now financially and where you want to go. I know this can sound like a complex existential question, so just keep it simple. Spend a little time evaluating all the financial pieces of your life. As mentioned earlier, this includes **Protections** (i.e., insurance for your home, other assets, income and life), your **Savings** (bank accounts, cash value life insurance) your **Growth** (personal development, business, real estate, stocks, bonds, etc.) your **Debt** (mortgages, loans) and your **Cash Flow** income, dividends, interest, loan payments, lifestyle expenses).

Most people don't look at these important areas holistically – but you should.

The LEAP framework introduced back in Chapter 1 can be very helpful here for gaining clarity. Furthermore, an experienced and qualified financial professional can suggest areas for improvement – and unproductive activities to curtail – that may not have occurred to you before.

Many people are not confident that they're doing all they can, financially speaking, for themselves and their families. All too often I see smart, successful people resign themselves to a mindset that their finances are too complicated or that the game is "rigged" against them. I know it seems that way sometimes, but this is exactly why you want to have a growth mindset. It will enable you to explore alternatives that could offer you more control of your financial future.

For many years, I felt the way many of you do about finances. As mentioned in Chapter 1, something that helped me tremendously on my journey to becoming a financial advisor was the Prosperity Economics Movement (PEM), which is about pulling back the curtain on how money really works and controlling your financial future from the driver's seat, not the passenger seat.

Financial Planning vs.	***Prosperity Economics***
Meets needs and goals only Based on limited ideas of "what you can afford."	Pursues wants and dreams Based on unlimited ideas of "what is possible?"
Minimizes requirements "How much do I have to save?"	Optimizes opportunities "How else can I build wealth?" mindset.
Product-oriented (what you buy) Focus is primarily on buying certain products.	Strategy-oriented (what you do) Based on time-tested principles and financial philosophies used to build wealth
Focused on rate-of-return "How much is this earning me?"	Focused on recovering opportunity cost Keep more money working for you
Institutions control your money Put your assets "under management," (and/or give control to government.)	You control your money Maintain responsibility for and access to your assets and funds.
Micro (vacuum) based Focus is on your "portfolio."	Macro (big picture) based View your whole personal economy
Net worth is measurement A bigger portfolio is the goal	Cash flow is measurement The goal is more money to enjoy each month
Retirement oriented Your reward for work is not working	Abundant/Freedom oriented Enjoy your work and your life – all life long.
Lives only on interest At mercy of interest rates, with fingers crossed you won't need to use principle	Spends and replaces principle A flexible, sustainable way to live
Money stays still Assets are accumulated into accounts where they sit, financially "stagnant."	Money moves Your personal economy is alive and well; money flows in and out of accounts.
Dollars do only one job Save separately for emergencies, education, retirement, major purchases. Spend each dollar for one purpose only.	Dollars do many jobs Dollars are used for flexible and multiple purposes.
Professional planner is the expert Finances are represented as something confusing that should be delegated.	Clients are empowered Money is demystified. Education-based approach builds financial confidence.

KEY LEARNINGS FROM CHAPTER 4:

- Mind the gap. Spending time and energy obsessing about what you ***haven't*** achieved (or acquired) in life prevents you from enjoying what you ***have*** achieved (and acquired).
- Research shows we tend to pay more attention to *negative events* than to positive events. We also tend to make decisions based on *negative outcomes and experiences*.
- Making a conscious effort to focus on the positive aspects of life can help you overcome challenges and put you in better position to withstand life's storms.
- Learn to develop an abundance mindset rather than a scarcity mindset.
- In our fast-moving unpredictable world, there are two essential things you can always control: your attitude and your effort.
- Becoming antifragile allows you to lean into disruptions in life rather than run away from them. With this approach, you will not only survive disruption but grow from it.

CONCLUSION

Remember my parents' journey to America that I described at the beginning of this book? It took tremendous courage to risk everything they had and come to this country from a vastly different culture, with little money in their pocket, and minimal mastery of English. While they overcame language barriers and prejudice to become successful professionals, there was one thing they never learned in all their years of schooling and professional practice: ***financial literacy***.

My parents' money mistakes were the catalyst that drove me to get my finances in order and to start sharing with people what I've learned about controlling wealth. I didn't realize this pursuit of financial literacy would also teach me how to have a more fulfilling and rewarding life overall.

Your financial journey will be filled with ups and downs. As with any journey, you'll make some missteps that, but these will provide Key Learnings and insights into your growth. Learning from other people's missteps (and their wisdom) will also increase your chances of success. As Eleanor Roosevelt once said, "Learn from the mistakes of others. You can't live long enough to make them all yourself."

My hope is that this guide will help you build a strong financial foundation that allows you to have a positive impact on your family, your community and the causes you support – an impact that lasts well after your time on this earth has passed.

Thanks again for making the commitment to read this guide. I hope the Key Steps and lessons I shared in this book will give you a new perspective on building wealth in all areas of your life – not just the financial areas. And I hope that years from now, you find yourself watching a stunning sunset on a beautiful beach and marveling at how you got so far in life. That would make me very happy.

"If we command our wealth, we shall be rich and free; if our wealth commands us, we are poor indeed." – Edmund Burke, Irish Economist and Philosopher

ABOUT THE AUTHOR

Tom Suvansri is the founder of *Perennial Pride*, where he focuses on comprehensive wealth management strategies that leverage sound economic principles to grow wealth with increased control and certainty. Tom has always had a passion for managing his family's wealth, and he continues to explore opportunities to protect and maximize each dollar.

His passion stems from witnessing the financial struggles of his parents, who ran a successful family physician practice. Unfortunately, his parents lacked the necessary financial education, which led them to lose control of their wealth and put their money at massive risk. As a result, much of the wealth they were able to create over their lifetime was not available for them to enjoy in their later years. The hardships Tom's parents endured throughout their lives motivated him to find a better path to prosperity and abundance for his family and clients. This drives Tom to continue to learn and grow so he can better serve the families, professionals and business owners he has the honor to help.

Tom graduated from The Pennsylvania State University with an MBA in finance after earning his BS in biology from The College of New Jersey. Prior to starting Perennial Pride, Tom spent 15 years in the pharmaceuticals industry, in various roles spanning corporate/commercial finance, marketing operations and compliance.

Born in Lower Merion, PA, and raised in Cherry Hill, NJ, Tom currently resides in Stamford, CT, with his wife, Bridget, and their two boys, Aidan and Colin. In his free time, Tom loves to read, exercise, play an occasional round of golf and just enjoy family time.

WORKSHEETS, EXERCISES, CHECKLISTS

HELPFUL RESOURCES

Important works that shaped my thinking
in the building of my financial and life philosophy.

Achor, Shawn - The Happiness Advantage

Brannan, Tammi - The Blueprint Process

Brown, Brene - Dare to Lead

Butler, Kim - Financial Planning Has Failed

Castiglione, Robert - Lifetime Economic Acceleration Process™

Corley, Tim - Rich Habits

Covey, Stephen - The Seven Habits of Highly Effective People

Elrod, Hal - The (6-minute) Miracle Morning

Frankl, Viktor - Man's Search for Meaning

Glason, George - The Richest Man in Babylon

Gunderson, Garrett - Killing Sacred Cows

Hardy, Darren - Design Your Best Year Ever

Hardy, Darren - The Compound Effect

Hill, Napoleon - Think and Grow Rich

Hogan, Bill - How Do You Eat an Elephant? One Bite at a Time

Holiday, Ryan - The Obstacle Is the Way/Ego Is the Enemy

Kelce, Jason - 2018 Super Bowl victory speech

Kiyosaki, Robert - Rich Dad Poor Dad

Lieber, Ron - The Opposite of Spoiled: Raising Kids Who Are Grounded, Generous, and Smart About Money

Nash, Nelson - Becoming Your Own Banker

Paradigm Life - The Hierarchy of Wealth

Sinek, Simon - Start with Why

Stanley, Thomas, and Danko, William - The Millionaire Next Door

Stinson, Nicolette - 10 Steps for Developing an Abundance Mindset

Sullivan, Dan - Strategic Coach

Taleb, Nassim - Antifragile

Visual Capitalist - The World's Most Influential Values

Ware, Bronnie - The Five Regrets of the Dying

Warner Brother Pictures - King Richard: American Dreams

Williams, Dr. Paige - Becoming AntiFragile: Learning to Thrive through Disruption, Challenge and Change

Winfrey, Oprah - Commencement Address to Class of 2012

Wright, Simon - The Power of Saying No

NOTES

NOTES

NOTES

CPSIA information can be obtained
at www.ICGtesting.com
Printed in the USA
BVHW030926120922
646800BV00016B/480

9 781088 045497